THREE THING

LIVING THE VIRTUES OF FAITH, HOPE AND LOVE IN THE SPIRIT OF THE SERVANT OF GOD:

BISHOP GUGLIELMO GIAQUINTA

Rev. Michael F. Murphy

Three Things That Last
©Michael F. Murphy 2015

Table of Contents

Acknowledgments

As any priest would admit, the homilies and conferences we give are often a synthesis of many sources, first and foremost, inspiration from the Holy Spirit. We also use ideas from sources we have read or heard in the course of our pastoral ministry. As we prepare a homily or retreat conference something will come to mind that we might have no idea where it came from but the Holy Spirit opened our hearts to it at that moment. These reflections were developed in just such a way. I have given credit to sources as I have known them. Other material I have picked up through 31 years of priestly ministry but cannot recall the sources. It is not my intention to plagiarize so if a source is not credited I thank the person from whom I might have received it and I am grateful to the Holy Spirit for providing it to me.

INTRODUCTION

The Heart of the Mystic

†*Jesus,*
  May your mind enlighten me,
  Your word guide me, your eyes follow me,
  Your ears listen to me, Your arms
  extended on the cross open me to
  universal love.

†*Jesus,*
  May Your crucified feet move me to
  give myself tirelessly for my
  brothers and sisters,
  may Your pierced heart be for me a
  source of grace for my journey and
  a place of rest in my weariness.

Amen.

(G. Giaquinta)

On Tuesday evening, February 9, 1818, Antoine Givre, a boy herding sheep in the Dombres region of France, had an unusual encounter. He met a priest striding toward him. He was pushing a rickety cart heaped with objects, among which he could make out a wooden headboard for a bed.

The priest called to the boy and asked if it was much further to a certain village. Antoine pointed out to him the modest little town before them which was disappearing into the darkness. "How small it is!" the priest murmured. Then he knelt on the frozen ground and prayed at length, his eyes fixed on the houses.

As he rose and set out again with his cart, the boy was at his side. When they arrived in front of the poor church, Fr. Jean Marie Vianney said to him: "Thank you for showing me the way to Ars...I will show you the way to heaven".[i]

This is a time of grace. You have been invited by the Lord to step away from your busy lives; to open our hearts and listen to His gentle, almost imperceptible voice. †Jesus is calling you to join Him on a journey of holiness.

Through the Sacred Scriptures, timeless mystical writings, and the reflections of the Servant of God, Bishop Guglielmo Giaquinta, you will be shown the way to heaven. You must make the choice to listen and follow.

We begin with words from the final book of Scripture, the Book of Revelation:

"I am the Alpha and the Omega, says the Lord, the One who is and who was and who is to come" (Rev. 1:8).

†Jesus is the beginning and the end of everything. †Jesus wants to surround us with His love, His life. But, is this what we want? We say we do; but are these empty words? †Jesus wants to be the beginning and end of my life. But, is †Jesus the beginning and end of all that I do? Is He the focus of every action; every word?

At the end of every liturgical year, we celebrate †Jesus as King; but, whose king? Is †Jesus my King, or someone else's? Pontius Pilate questioned †Jesus as a king. But †Jesus made it clear: *"My kingdom is not here"*. †Jesus was not Pilate's king. Caesar was Pilate's king. †Jesus was not the alpha and omega of Pontius Pilate.

Before I can truthfully say, †Jesus Christ is King, I must decide: to what kingdom do I belong? Is this world the beginning and end for me? In this world I want everything I can get. There are ways I can build my own little kingdom here. I can build my kingdom using worldly resources. I can also build my own kingdom of piety and spirituality; one that has nothing to do with the Word of God. Creating and worshipping a Kingdom of my own making. Many Christians build religious kingdoms that have little resemblance to the Way, the Truth, and the Life. Spiritual kingdoms they control. Or, do I recognize myself simply as a pilgrim in this world; patiently traveling through it? I am on my way to the Kingdom that †Jesus promised. The Kingdom that †Jesus died for; as St. Paul reminds us: recognizing our citizenship in heaven. My citizenship is revealed in where I set my heart. If my heart is set on the world, †Jesus is not my king, any more than He was a king for Pontius Pilate. †Jesus is my King when my heart is set on His Kingdom. What kind of heart is set on the Kingdom of Heaven?

It begins with a **Silent Heart.** This is a heart open to gentle God's presence in prayer. A silent heart is listening for the voice of the King; a heart that is nurtured in solitude. Daily, I retreat from the noise and busyness of life to waste time with †Jesus; to go away with Him, even if ever so briefly.

"We must become accustomed to let Him talk, and desire to learn how to listen to Him...We must always be listening for His voice, ready to give ourselves to Him. The person unable to be silent with others cannot hear the voice of the Master".[ii]

If you haven't already done so now is chance to discover that **Silent Heart** within. Or, maybe, rediscover it.

The People of God's Kingdom also possess a **Repentant Heart.** When I possess a repentant heart I recognize my sinfulness. I take responsibility for my mistakes. It is a heart that does not take God's mercy for granted. I have now become aware of the new life I have been blessed with. I actively work for the on-going conversion of my life. I am no longer content with minimalism and mediocrity in my life. I am now choosing to love with <u>all</u> that I am.

When Christ is my King, I have a **Heart that Cries Out.**

This is a heart that cries out to be transformed into the Sacred Heart of †Jesus; a heart that loves to the maximum. I am now striving to love God with 'all my heart, all my soul, all my strength and all my mind and to love my neighbor as myself'. I desire to be in the image and likeness of God. My passion is to cry out like St. Paul:

"Yet, I live, no longer I, but Christ lives in me" (Gal. 2: 19).

A heart set on the Kingdom of Christ †Jesus is a **Remembering Heart**. Never forgetting the love God has shown to me. I always remember His goodness to me. In times of desolation I remember the consolation the Lord has given me. These memories give me courage to endure the crosses that appear in my life. In my heart I remember that I belong to a pilgrim people. My citizenship is not of this world. I am being led beyond this world.

"He is the door and the way to eternal life; it is up to us to follow Him. Up, ever upward, He leads us to the perfection of the Father: 'You, therefore, are to be perfect, even as your Heavenly Father is perfect (Matt. 5:48)".[iii]

The remembering heart never forgets that †Jesus is my King, my Lord. I am ready to do all for the glory and honor of God.

A heart set on the Kingdom is a **Desirous Heart.** My heart's greatest desire is holiness: to become a saint. In the Psalms we read:

"Holiness befits your house, O Lord, for length of days" (Ps. 93: 5).

Do we desire God's Kingdom; the house of the Lord? It can only be entered through the door of holiness. The desirous heart seeks God's will alone; surrendering my will to live His.

"Our renunciation, at least our interior renunciation, must be complete in order for us to be able to walk on the way of perfection".[iv]

This desire leads to a **Docile Heart.** This is a heart that does not seek its own power. It is to possess the heart of †Jesus who, rather than be served, came to serve others. This is where most of us differ from †Jesus. We choose to use a power **not** ours to use. To judge, reject or use others. Jesus chose **not** to exercise a power He had a legitimate right to command. He chose to be the docile servant. He chose to surrender to the will of the Father. He chose to live after the manner of His Blessed Mother who responded to the invitation of the angel Gabriel with the words:

"Behold, I am the maidservant of the Lord. May it be done to me according to your word" (Luke 1: 38).

A heart set on †Jesus is a **Eucharistic Heart.** It is a heart filled with gratitude. The word "Eucharist" comes from the Greek word meaning "thanksgiving". Regardless of whether the blessings from God are great or small, I am one with the Eucharistic Heart of †Jesus. I live with a grateful heart.

A Eucharistic Heart is also a **Sacrificial Heart**. I am willing to be broken and poured out as †Jesus was for me. A sacrificial heart never cries out in times of trial or tribulation: "Why me, Lord?" In gratitude, it prays: "Why am I so loved?" Why am I so loved to be worthy to unite myself to the sufferings of †Jesus?

†Jesus said to His disciples:

"Store up treasure in heaven, where neither moth nor decay destroys, nor thieves break in and steal. For where your treasure is, there also will your heart be" (Matthew 6: 20-21).

Our Kingdom is where our heart is. Who is my King, my Lord, my God? Toward what Kingdom am I traveling? It is in prayer that we know the way. Bishop Giaquinta reminds us:

"If we tried to make a comparison between active and contemplative life, we would side with †Jesus who defended Mary by saying to Martha, 'Mary has chosen the better part' (Luke 10: 42)". ᵛ

In chapters 10 and 11 of Luke's Gospel we find †Jesus teaching His disciples about prayer. We are privileged to listen in to this teaching. When asked by his disciples to teach them to pray as John taught his disciples, †Jesus simply shares with them His own prayer.

"Our Father, who art in heaven, hallowed be your name. Your Kingdom come, your will be done, on earth as it is in heaven..."

During a visit to the home of Lazarus, Martha and Mary, †Jesus teaches another important lesson (Luke 10: 38-42). He told Martha, that Mary had chosen the better part by sitting at His feet and listening to Him. But this can't be the limit of our spiritual life. Both Martha and Mary are needed. Prayer and good works are essential for growth in holiness.

Teresa of Avila reminds us that prayer and service are two sisters, like Martha and Mary:

"Be occupied in prayer not for the sake of our enjoyment but as to have this strength to serve. Let's refuse to take an unfamiliar path, for we shall get lost at the most opportune time. It would indeed be novel to think of having these favors from God through a path other than the one He took and the one followed by all the saints. May the thought never enter our minds. Believe me, Martha and Mary must join together in order to show hospitality to the Lord and have Him always present and not host Him badly by failing to give Him something to eat. How would Mary, always seated at His feet, provide Him with food if her sister did not help her? His food is that in every possible way we draw souls that they may be saved and praise Him always".[vi]

†Jesus also told the parable of the Good Samaritan (Luke 10: 29-37). The priest and the Levite were on their way to prayer. But they did not practice charity. They left the man who had been robbed along the side of the road.

†Jesus also teaches the importance of persistence in prayer. We are to pray always.

"Ask and you shall receive. Seek and you shall find. Knock and it will be opened to you" (Matthew 11: 9).

†Jesus saves the most important lesson for the end of the discourse (Luke 11: 9-13): the importance of faith and trust in God. We will not always get what we are praying for. How will we respond to this? This saying has been attributed to Fr. Karl Rahner:

"The Christian of the future will either by a mystic or not exist at all."

The mystic looks beyond the physical, beyond the obvious. The mystic sees the hidden things of God. A mystic understand that God...

"will not give us a snake when we ask for a fish or a scorpion when we ask for an egg" (Luke 11:11-12).

The mystic understand that the answer to some of our prayers is **"no"**.

There are many Christians, probably most, who live an <u>ideology</u> of Christianity. They do not live an authentic Christianity. The Levite and the priest in the parable of the Good Samaritan practiced the ideology of Judaism. They followed the Law faithfully. They could not defile themselves for prayer by touching the wounded and bleeding man. The Samaritan was the true child of God. He was a child of Abraham, Isaac and Jacob. A Christian at prayer accepts the hidden things of God. The Christian mystic does not have to have a reason why their prayer wasn't answered as they expected. The Mystic understand that faith is both knowledge and love. Christianity is not about following a doctrine. It is about falling in love with God. When a husband and wife fall in love, they trust one another. When a child loves a parent, they trust that parent. If we are in love with God, we will trust God. We will allow ourselves to rest in the palm of His hand. We will imitate the love of God.

"If the Father and †Jesus, the Incarnate Word, love people so much, can we believe that we have a true interior life without effectively participating in this love?" [vii]

In †Jesus' own personal prayer, which he taught to His disciples, He prayed: *"Thy will be done"*. We say this at every Mass; every time we pray the Lord's Prayer. To say, *"Thy will be done"* and to <u>believe</u> it are two different things. It is the difference between the mystic and the ideological, non-trusting Christian. *"Pray always"*, St. Paul wrote. But pray with the heart of a mystic. Pray with the heart of one who is in love with God. One who trusts God even when He says "no". The mystic at prayer imitates †Jesus. In the garden of Gethsemane, †Jesus prayed to "Abba" to let the cup of suffering pass Him by. But, the Father said "no". When He was nailed to the cross, the crowd jeered at Him and said: *"If you are the son of God, come down from the Cross and end your suffering"* (cf: Luke 24:37). †Jesus said "no".

Open your hearts in prayer to listen to the voice of the Lord. You will hear Him in the Scriptures, in the timeless wisdom of the Church and her mystical writers and in the stillness of your heart. Embrace the **Silent Heart**, approach the Lord with a **Repentant Heart**, and a **Heart That Cries Out** to be transformed into the image of the loving heart of †Jesus, and His plans for you. Let your **Heart Remember** the love God has for you and, with a **Desirous Heart**, thirst for holiness. With a **Docile Heart**, embrace the heart of †Jesus. Pray for a **Eucharistic Heart**. If the Lord is asking you to accept a **Sacrificial Heart**, respond as Mary did: *"Let it be done to me as you say"*.

It is the heart of the mystic that embraces the fullness of love. A heart that strives to be: holy as God is holy.

1. FAITH

Faith Along The Way

Act of Faith

O my God, I firmly believe
That you are one God in three divine persons,
Father, Son, and Holy Spirit.
I believe that your divine Son became man
and died for our sins and that He will come
to judge the living and the dead.
I believe these and all the truths which
the Holy Catholic Church teaches because
you revealed them who are eternal truth and
wisdom, who can neither deceive not be
deceived. In this faith I intend to live and die.
Amen.

"†*Jesus and his disciples set out for the villages of Caesarea Philippi. Along the way he asked his disciples, 'Who do people say that I am?' They said in reply, 'John the Baptist, others Elijah, still others one of the prophets.' And he asked them, 'But who do you say that I am?' Peter said* to him in reply, 'You are the Christ.' Then he warned them not to tell anyone about him" (Mark 8: 27-30).

To fully understand this passage from Mark's Gospel, we must recall what occurred prior to this incident. †Jesus and His disciples had just left Bethsaida. There, †Jesus had cured a blind man. You might remember that this cure had taken place in three stages: the man was blind when he approached †Jesus; †Jesus put saliva on his eyes and he could partially see. The man remarked that *"people looked like walking trees"* (Mark 8: 24); finally, †Jesus put His hands on the man's eyes a second time. The man could then see clearly. Mark writes:

"His sight was restored and he could see everything distinctly" (Mark 8:25).

That is the background to what then occurs at Caesarea Philippi. Mark writes:

"†Jesus and His disciples set out for the villages of Caesarea Philippi. Along the way, He asked His disciples: 'Who do people say that I am?'" (Mark 8: 27).

Mark tells us that *"along the way"*, †Jesus asked His disciples a question. Obviously, they are on a journey. The disciples are on a journey to Jerusalem with †Jesus. But they are also on a journey to faith in †Jesus. When †Jesus put saliva on the blind man's eyes, it produced only partial sight. It was here, at Caesarea Philippi, we have

Peter's confession of †Jesus as Messiah. But, his profession of faith simply witnesses to his <u>partial</u> sight of †Jesus. Peter believed in a culturally, religiously and historically conditioned meaning of Messiah: a Davidic king who will liberate the Jewish people from the Romans who were currently occupying their country. At this point, the disciples are ONLY capable of partial and imperfect belief. Peter is correct when he confesses †Jesus as the Christ. But, like the second stage of the cure of the blind man they encountered in Bethsaida, Peter is only partially correct. His eyes are not fully open to the complete truth about †Jesus.

There is a deeper mystery to †Jesus as Messiah. The disciples have not yet come to full sight and understanding. They are not seeing everything clearly; just as the blind man from Bethsaida could not see clearly; at least at first.

†Jesus then broaches the deeper mystery.

"He began to tell them that the Son of Man must suffer greatly and be rejected by the elders, the chief priests and the scribes and be killed and rise after three days" (Mark 8: 31).

The disciples are *"on the way"* to full sight. Full sight will happen in Jerusalem when they witness the passion, death and resurrection of †Jesus. Now, they see only partially. At Caesarea Philippi, Peter could not accept the fullness of the mystery that †Jesus was preparing them for. So, he took †Jesus aside and began to rebuke Him. He began to argue with †Jesus. At this point on their journey to discipleship, the Twelve had much to learn. They had no clue what it meant to be an Apostle of Holiness. The other followers of †Jesus also had much to learn. They saw †Jesus as a prophet: John the Baptist or Elijah; one who would usher in the Messianic era with temporal power and economic prosperity. Even though the disciples see †Jesus as the Christ they still demonstrate only <u>partial</u> sight. Yet, they criticize other people who see †Jesus only as one of the prophets. They think they are better because they recognize †Jesus as the "Christ". The Messiah-ship of †Jesus involves rejection, suffering, death and Resurrection. This is the true picture; the complete picture. The fullness of sight, the fullness of faith, comes when we can participate in the paschal mystery.

†Jesus responds to Peter's rebuke by calling Peter "satan": *"Get behind me satan"*. The name "satan" originates from the Aramaic word "sa'tana". It refers to a "stumbling block" or a "barrier". †Jesus and His disciples are *"on the way"*. But, Peter is blocking that way. He is trying to hold †Jesus back from completing the purpose for which He put aside His divinity and took human form as St. Paul reminds us in his beautiful Philippians' hymn.

"He emptied Himself, taking the form of a slave, coming in human likeness and found human in appearance" (Phil. 2: 7).

Peter is rejecting †Jesus' acceptance of God's plan. †Jesus says to Peter: *"Get behind me!"* The vocation of the disciple of holiness is to get behind †Jesus.

"Whoever wishes to come after me, must deny himself, take up his cross, and follow me" (Mark 8: 34).

As †Jesus rejected the idea of messianic glory and embraced the suffering of the cross, so must the disciple. The Christian life is more than just intellectual ascent. We read in the letter of James:

"Faith, of itself, if it does not have works, is dead" (James 2: 17).

To see †Jesus only as the messiah, is to possess only partial sight, partial faith. To see †Jesus as suffering servant, is to see the fullness of His mission. To participate in His suffering is to believe fully. It is to possess a deeper faith. Faith without good works witnesses to partial sight. Living our faith and expressing our faith through good works and through sacrifice, shows fullness of sight. We must understand that the fullness of love cannot be separated from faith. The call to holiness is the call to full sight; to take up the cross and follow †Jesus; faith AND good works (James 2: 14-17).

"You believe that God is One. You do well. Even the demons believe that and tremble" (James 2: 19).

James makes it clear: our faith must be greater than that of demons.

Are we *"on the way"*? Have we truly accepted the invitation of †Jesus? Do we selflessly live our Catholic faith for all to see? Do we follow the instruction found in the Letter of James? Faith AND good works. Bishop Giaquinta writes:

"It is not enough to live in a position of theoretical love; rather, it is necessary that this love be made practical...that is, we must really try to understand the difficulties that beset so many of our brothers and sisters and empathize with their anxieties – this is the first act of charity. However, we will not be able to do this if instead of reflecting on the mentality of our times...we waste time moralizing, which is a very easy thing to do but also perfectly useless. Instead, we must try to meet with an open (mind) and an ever more open heart, the demands of our troubled world" [viii]

Peter was moralizing. He and the others were not willing to accept the full vision of the mission of †Jesus. Instead, they tried to protect their image of †Jesus. Peter was a *"stumbling block"*, a *"barrier"* ("sa'tana"). He was not ready to participate fully in the mission of †Jesus. Is our response to the call to holiness a full or partial response?

Do we respond in the minimum or to the maximum? Are we *"on the way"* to fullness of sight?

Reflect on your response to the call to holiness. Explore how you witness to discipleship in your faith community. Some begin with only partial sight. Some will end the same way. Others desire to be "on the way" to holiness; to fullness of sight. Their faith is expressed in words and actions: love, sacrifice and self-gift. But this demands going out of our self. It means moving beyond our comfort zone; serving †Jesus by serving others. Bishop Giaquinta reminds us of our place in God's plan:

"We must remain in the world in order to know its pain, to heal the pain, and so offer words of compassion to people in need... If we do not wish to be left behind and feel terribly outdated, it is indispensable that we stay in touch with the world. As the world changes, so must our apostolic methods. As the needs of the world are new, so our methods must also be new". [ix]

If we are truly *"on the way"* with †Jesus, our life is one of movement with the Holy Spirit. We cannot be paralyzed by the fear of change. We cannot be fossilized in the past, using the excuse: "We've always done it that way". We must possess "the courage of the truth" as Bishop Giaquinta wrote in describing Jonah who was *"on the way"* to Nineveh to preach repentance to the people. Bishop Giaquinta possessed a "fullness of sight". He was a man of vision because he was a man of faith. He was promoting the universal call to holiness long before it was taught by the Second Vatican Council in Chapter Five on the Dogmatic Constitution of the Church (_Lumen Gentium_). He was willing to participate in the Paschal Mystery in his own life. I recall the efforts of many people donating blood for him. I once travelled to Tivoli to celebrate Mass for him in his bedroom because he was too weak to get out of bed or even turn the pages of the Roman Missal or raise the chalice.

The various Institutes and the Pro Sanctity Movement are for those "on the way". For those who are not afraid to walk the journey of holiness. We should not live our Christian life as a blur. Our Christian life cannot be out of focus. We must constantly strive for the fullness of sight. We are called to follow the way of †Jesus, His disciples and the saints. †Jesus leads us to see Him clearly as we read in Psalm 116:

"I will walk before the Lord, in the land of the living" (Vs. 9).

As †Jesus and the disciples continued their journey to Jerusalem, we read, in Mark's Gospel, chapter 9, of the Transfiguration. After the magnificent event on the mountain, the evangelist Mark tells us what happened next:

"As †Jesus came down from the mountain with Peter, James, John and approached the other disciples, they saw a large crowd around them and scribes arguing with them. Immediately on seeing him, the whole crowd was utterly amazed. They ran up to him and greeted him. He asked them, 'What are you arguing about with them?' Someone *from the crowd answered him, 'Teacher, I have brought to you my son possessed by a mute spirit. Whenever it seizes him, it throws him down; he foams at the mouth, grinds his teeth, and becomes rigid. I asked your disciples to drive it out, but they were unable to do so.'*

"He said to them in reply, 'O faithless generation, how long will I be with you? How long will I endure you? Bring him to me.' They brought the boy to him. And when he saw him, the spirit immediately threw the boy into convulsions. As he fell to the ground, he began to roll around and foam at the mouth. Then he questioned his father, 'How long has this been happening to him?' He replied, 'Since childhood. It has often thrown him into fire and into water to kill him. But if you can do anything, have compassion on us and help us.' †Jesus said to him, 'If you can!' Everything is possible to one who has faith.' Then the boy's father cried out, 'I do believe, help my unbelief!' †Jesus, on seeing a crowd rapidly gathering, rebuked the unclean spirit and said to it, 'Mute and deaf spirit, I command you: come out of him and never enter him again!'" (Mark 9: 14-25).

†Jesus declares to the crowd: *"O faithless generation, how long will I be with you?"* (Mark 9: 19). Is †Jesus speaking of the scribes and Pharisees? Is †Jesus speaking of the people of Israel? Actually, †Jesus is speaking to twelve individuals: His Apostles. The Twelve had shown an increasing lack of faith on this journey. This is seen in their inability to affect a cure of this boy who is possessed.

Lately, it has been all about them; what **they** can do. Recall when they returned from their mission as recorded in chapter 6 of Mark's Gospel:

"All the disciples gathered together with †Jesus and reported <u>all</u> <u>that</u> <u>they</u> <u>had</u> <u>done</u> and taught" (Mark 6: 30).

Did the disciples give the credit to God? NO! They did not say: *'look what we did through the power of God'.* Now, they cannot understand why they had been able to cure before, and cannot do it now? The disciples were becoming increasingly self-sufficient. They were showing an arrogance that was displayed in believing they knew better than †Jesus. Recall, prior to this episode, was Peter's profession of faith and rebuke by †Jesus. We contrast this self-sufficiency of the disciples with the father in the Gospel who approaches †Jesus seeking a cure for his possessed son. This man recognizes his lack of faith.

"I do believe, help my unbelief" (Mark 9:24).

This brings to mind the Syro-Phonecian woman who, two chapters earlier in Mark's Gospel (Mark 7: 24-30), expressed her lack of worthiness as she sought a cure for her daughter. She was asking only for the crumbs from the table of the Chosen.

"Lord, even the dogs under the table eat the children's scraps" (Mark 7: 28).

This father asks †Jesus to help him in his failure, his weak faith. He turned to †Jesus in His nothingness, just as the woman had. The Twelve are not turning to †Jesus in their weakness. They are trying to figure out why they could cure people previously, but now, can't!

How often do we get caught up in our self-sufficiency? We live in a culture that glorifies independence. If prayers are not answered the way we want, we have the means to take matters into our own hands. We slowly insulate ourselves from trusting in God by looking to the world and our culture for answers and solutions. Bishop Giaquinta directs us to another way:

"We wish to reach the highest degree of our self-giving by detaching ourselves from all that is not related to God. This is what the spirit of poverty consists of. It is not a matter of mere material renunciation from something tangible, but an interior renunciation from everything, even the noblest things, such as spiritual things, forms of devotion, if necessary. †Jesus said it clearly: 'In the same way, every one of you who does not renounce all his possessions, cannot be my disciple (Luke 14: 33)". [x]

Here, the Founder is consistent with the teachings of the great mystical writers including Teresa of Avila, John of the Cross and the author of The Cloud of Unknowing.

Because of their lack of faith, lack of spiritual poverty and hardness of heart, the disciples were unable to perform miracles. They were unable to act as disciples of †Jesus. When they asked why they could not cast out the demon, †Jesus says to them:

"This kind can only come out through prayer" (Mark 9: 29).

The disciples must re-direct their attention to God. They do not drive out demons, God does. We must turn to God in faith and prayer if we hope to be successful disciples of †Jesus; if we desire to be Apostles of holiness. Now is the time to re-direct our attention to God. We must not wait any longer. Our faith must be expressed in our daily life by how we embrace the Cross of Christ. Now is the time to truly embrace our call to holiness; to be saints. You can do it! As †Jesus says to the father of the possessed boy:

"Everything is possible to the one who has faith" (Mark 9: 23).

Faith and Full Sight

I believe in you, Father,
God-Love who love us infinitely
and wish a full response
of love from each of us.

I thank you for your Son,
†Jesus Christ, the eternal Word made
man, our brother
who with his life, death and resurrection
did not only save us, but made us new.

Give us the Spirit of love
who leads us to live out your message.
form is us the face of your Son:
who will give us the strength
to extend your invitation of holiness
to all people.

(+G. Giaquinta)

It has been quite a journey for †Jesus and His disciples from Galilee to Jerusalem. Along the way, we have witnessed failure; failure on the part of the Twelve.

They refused to grasp the mission of †Jesus. †Jesus could not have been clearer about what awaited Him in Jerusalem. Three times he predicted His passion. Three times they failed to listen. The Twelve were more concerned about themselves; about their future.

Earlier, we reflected on that moment in Caesarea Philippi. There, Peter failed †Jesus when he boasted of how he would prevent any harm coming to the Lord. In response, †Jesus calls Peter *"satan"*; a stumbling block, a barrier to God's plan. This occurred after the first passion prediction by †Jesus. After a second Passion prediction, it is John who fails †Jesus.

"John said to Him: 'Teacher, we saw someone driving out demons in your name, and we tried to prevent him because he does not follow us'. †Jesus replied, 'Do not prevent him. There is no one who performs a mighty deed in my name who can at the same time speak ill of me. For whoever is not against us is for us'" (Mark 10: 38-40).

John told †Jesus to stop someone from casting out demons. That person was not part of their company. †Jesus responded, *"Whoever is not against us is for us"*. John had failed to understand the mission of †Jesus: to reconcile the whole world to the Father, not just a privileged few.

A third time on the journey, †Jesus said He would be handed over to the chief priests and condemned to death.

"They were on the way, going up to Jerusalem, and †Jesus went ahead of them. They were amazed, and those who followed were afraid. Taking the Twelve aside again, he began to tell them what was going to happen to him.

'Behold, we are going up to Jerusalem, and the Son of Man will be handed over to the chief priests and the scribes, and they will condemn him to death and hand him over to the Gentiles who will mock him, spit upon him, scourge him, and put him to death, but after three days he will rise.'

Then James and John, the sons of Zebedee, came to him and said to him, 'Teacher, we want you to do for us whatever we ask of you.'

He replied, 'What do you wish (me) to do for you?'

They answered him, 'Grant that in your glory we may sit one at your right and the other at your left.'

†Jesus said to them, 'You do not know what you are asking. Can you drink the cup that I drink or be baptized with the baptism with which I am baptized?'

They said to him, 'We can.' †Jesus said to them, 'The cup that I drink, you will drink, and with the baptism with which I am baptized, you will be baptized; but to sit at my right or at my left is not mine to give but is for those for whom it has been prepared'" (Mark 10: 32-40).

James and John ask †Jesus if they can sit on His right and left. Imagine the arrogance and ambition of these two brothers. What †Jesus had just said about His upcoming Passion, went right over their heads. Again, His disciples failed. They failed to listen and grasp His words. They were too concerned about their future. There is no recognition of what will <u>happen to</u> †Jesus in Jerusalem. They want

†Jesus to make things <u>happen</u> <u>for</u> <u>them</u> in Jerusalem. So, instead, they plot to be in powerful positions.

Six verses later, when †Jesus and His disciples are only a few miles from Jerusalem, we read of an incident involving a blind man named Bartimaeus:

"As †Jesus was leaving Jericho with his disciples and a sizable crowd, Bartimaeus, a blind man, the son of Timaeus, sat by the roadside begging. On hearing that it was †Jesus of Nazareth, he began to cry out and say, '†Jesus, son of David, have pity on me.' And many rebuked him, telling him to be silent. But he kept calling out all the more, 'Son of David, have pity on me.' †Jesus stopped and said, 'Call him.' So they called the blind man, saying to him, 'Take courage; get up, †Jesus is calling you.' He threw aside his cloak, sprang up, and came to †Jesus. †Jesus said to him in reply, 'What do you want me to do for you?' The blind man replied to him, 'Master, I want to see.' †Jesus told him, 'Go your way; your faith has saved you.' Immediately he received his sight and followed him <u>on the way</u>." (Mark 10: 46-52).

We meet Bartimaeus; a blind man. This blind man will put the disciples to shame. On this journey from Galilee to Jerusalem the disciples have been witnesses to the awesome power of †Jesus. †Jesus had raised the daughter of Jairus from the dead (Mark 6: 35-43). At the Sea of Galilee, †Jesus had fed 5,000 people with five loaves and two fish (Mark 6: 34-44). He was transfigured before their eyes, conversing with Moses and Elijah (Mark 9:2-8). Bartimaeus has seen none of this. In fact, he sees nothing! We come across this man who is both <u>*blind*</u> and <u>*sitting by*</u>

the side of the road.   These two facts indicate his insignificance in the eyes of the world: he is blind AND a beggar.   He is no one of importance.   Bartimaeus, enthusiastically, calls out to †Jesus: _"†Jesus, Son of David, have pity on me"_ (Mark 10: 47).   He doesn't care what people think as he praises †Jesus; referring to †Jesus as _"Son of David"._   Many in the crowd rebuke him for his outburst.   But, he will not let the crowd silence him as he praises †Jesus and calls out to Him.   †Jesus then says to those near Him: _"Call him"._ These are significant words: _"Call him"._   Recall how Peter, James and John left their nets when †Jesus _called them._   The same three apostles Mark has just described as failing †Jesus.   Those three left their nets, their trade, their possessions, and their father immediately to follow †Jesus.   Mark tells us that Bartimaeus jumped up _"immediately"._   But, the blind man surpasses the response of the first disciples.   He throws off his cloak; his only vestige of dignity.   He presents himself to †Jesus with nothing.   He has completely humbled himself before †Jesus.

What a contrast we see.   The disciples have increasingly searched for authority, power and security; Bartimaeus only wants †Jesus.   †Jesus asks Bartimaeus the same question He asked James and John earlier (in vs. 36): _"What do you want me to do for you?"_ (Mark 10: 51). The sons of Zebedee asked for position and power. Bartimaeus simply asks to see.   The disciples, with all they have seen, remain partially blind to the messianic mission of †Jesus. Yet, Bartimaeus, from the beginning, recognized †Jesus as Messiah; referring to Him as *"Son of David"*. What Bartimaeus already possessed, has eluded the Twelve: the link between faith and sight. Bartimaeus possessed both: faith and spiritual insight.

†Jesus says to Bartimaeus: *"Go your way, your faith has made you well"* (Mark 10: 52). His unconditional commitment to †Jesus is the catalyst for the miracle, giving him full sight. His physical sight is a manifestation of what he already sees in his heart through faith. He sees †Jesus as the Son of God. Bartimaeus became a disciple of †Jesus, that day. In the Gospel: *"Immediately, he received his sight and followed †Jesus on the way"* (Mark 10: 52); on the way to Jerusalem. Bartimaeus is presented as a true disciple. He is prepared to follow the way of †Jesus: through the cross...to the empty tomb; from suffering and death...to Resurrection. The story of Bartimaeus stands in stark contrast to the failure of the disciples. Those that have faith in †Jesus will see the truth. The Twelve did not yet possess this.

Do we take our access to †Jesus for granted? Has it blinded us to the truth? We enjoy comfort and security in our relationship with †Jesus. We have the Sacred Scriptures, the Sacraments, and the teachings of the Church, and the timeless wisdom of the mystics and great spiritual writers of the Catholic tradition. We are able to converse with God in prayer. But are we blind to the truth of where these gifts lead us? The Christian spiritual life only matures on the way of the Cross; through acts of self-gift, surrender and sacrifice. Bishop Giaquinta reminds us:

"We look to †Jesus to complete our transformation in the beatific vision of Heaven, yet we must start heaven on earth now by the greatest effort possible in imitating the life and virtues of the Lord. Union with Him will come through the death of the 'old (self)', the result of mortification, and through particular virtues practiced in our daily life...Humility is first among all the virtues. Root it deeply in your heart if you wish to take even the smallest step on the road to perfection" [xi].

Clearly, Peter, James and John lacked humility. Bartimaeus didn't care about reputation or personal dignity. He wanted to be with †Jesus. Bartimaeus wanted to follow †Jesus wherever He went. What did James and John want? Places of authority and to sit on His right and on His left. Peter wanted to be the great protector of †Jesus. Those that possess true faith see the Cross of Christ as the Way, the Truth and the Life. True disciples follow the way of †Jesus, even when the way leads to Jerusalem, even when it takes them to a place of sacrifice and surrender. When †Jesus is transfigured – I want to be there. When †Jesus feeds 5,000 - I want to be there. When †Jesus cries out in agony on the cross - I must want to be there, too.

As †Jesus approached Jerusalem, we read in John's Gospel:

"Many of His disciples returned to their former way of life, and no longer accompanied Him" (John 6:66).

These were no casual observers who walked away. They were committed believers. They had faith in †Jesus as Messiah. They were disciples. But they did not possess fullness of sight. These disciples had witnessed remarkable things: †Jesus changing water into wine at Cana; †Jesus curing people of diseases and disabilities; †Jesus multiplying loaves and fish. They saw †Jesus walking on water. After all this, they still decided to leave Him. What did †Jesus do wrong? †Jesus did nothing wrong. It was something that He said:

"I am the living bread come down from Heaven; whoever eats this bread will live forever...Do not work for food that perishes, but for the food that endures for eternal life" (cf: John 6: 35-59).

These disciples knew †Jesus wasn't referring to cannibalism, but something far too difficult for them to do. †Jesus was talking about powerlessness: being devoured as bread; being broken; being poured out as wine. Some of His disciples could not accept this. Even after all the miracles and hope-filled words †Jesus had spoken to them. Yet, they misunderstood the power of †Jesus. They understood His power only in earthly terms. God's power is different from the world's power. The Scriptures describe it with the Greek word: "ex-ousia". It is not the power of muscle, speed or brilliance. God's power lies at the deeper moral and spiritual levels. God's power does not have: the speed or muscle of an Olympic athlete, the physical beauty of a movie star or the gifted speech of an orator. Muscle, swiftness, beauty, brilliance and grace all reflect God's glory. But they are not the way God shows power in the world. Have you ever been slapped by someone and were powerless to defend yourself? Then you know how God feels in the world; especially when we defy His will; when we use His gifts for personal gain. Have you ever cried tears and felt shame at your own inadequacy? Then you have felt how God feels in the world; especially when He can't make us change; when He can't break through our stony hearts. Have you ever been cursed for your goodness by people who misunderstood you and you were powerless to make them see things your way? Then you have felt how God feels in the world; especially when prayers are not answered the way we want them to be answered and we become angry with God.

God never forces Himself on us. God's power is more muted, more helpless, more marginalized. It is why †Jesus said,

"Blessed are the meek...Blessed are the lowly...Blessed are those who hunger and thirst for righteousness" (cf: Matthew 5: 1-12).

God's power lies at a much deeper level. God's power will, in the end, have the final say. In the world's scheme of things survival of the fittest is the rule. This is the way to get ahead and win. In God's scheme of things survival of the weakest is the rule. We must be weak enough to be a disciple of holiness. The disciple looks for the prize at the end of the race. Disciples run the race with faith in their hearts. Many in the company of †Jesus could not accept this. It is among the weak that we will find God.

"Gradually, the soul has a new vision of reality. She savors in a new, complete way that she has always known but what is suddenly seen in a different light and experienced in a new way...Her only desire is for God Himself to teach her about revealed truth. She desires to deepen supernatural principles within herself...to value everything only in relation to eternity and to the great principles of God and revelation". [xii]

St. Paul wrote:

"Be subordinate to one another...wives to husbands...husbands love your wives as Christ loved the Church" (cf: Ephesians 5: 21-30).

When St. Paul wrote of *"subordinate"*, it is not in terms of power; one person having power over another. Rather, Paul defines it in terms of sacrificial love: to surrender myself as †Jesus did; to choose to be bread that is broken rather than a force to be reckoned with. The struggle for power and domination comes by using muscle, popularity, and brilliance. As Christians, as disciples of holiness, our weapons are: faith, hope, love, personal integrity, prayer. Bishop Giaquinta often spoke of the "violence of love". We are to become "revolutionaries". We are to be "revolutionaries of love".

Many of †Jesus' disciples could not accept Him as bread to be consumed by the powerful. They could not accept powerlessness. What kind of power do you feed upon: Possessions, popularity, control? The need to be obeyed or listened too? Is the way of †Jesus too demanding? Are His words too difficult to consume? We have nothing to fear by placing our faith in †Jesus. St Anthony of Padua preached:

"In Isaiah the Lord says: 'I have written you in my hands' (49: 16). Note that for writing three things are necessary: paper, ink and pen. The hands of Christ were the paper as it were; His blood the ink; the nails the pen. Christ has inscribed us in His hands, therefore, for three distinct reasons: (1) to show the scars of the wounds he bore for us to the Father, thus inviting the Father to show us mercy. (2) In order not to forget us. For this reason, He says in Isaiah: *'Can a woman forget her infant, and not have pity on the son of her womb? And if she should forget you, behold, I have written you in my hands'* (49: 15-16). (3) He has written in His hands what kind of people we should be and in whom we should believe. 'Do not be faithless', therefore...O Christian, 'but be instead a believer'". [xiii]

42

†Jesus asked those who remain: *"Do you also want to leave?"* (John 6: 67). This question can be addressed to us. Oh, we would not leave the Church. But, we are unwilling to become what we receive in Holy Communion? Maybe we are content to be interested followers of †Jesus, but not His disciples; not apostles of holiness; that would be too demanding; costing far too much. The apostle of holiness believes †Jesus has the words of eternal life. The apostle of holiness "believes what he reads, teaches others what he believes, and practices what he teaches" (Rite of Ordination). These words from the Rite of Ordination apply to us all, whether we are of the ordained priesthood or of the common priesthood of the faithful. The apostle of holiness believes that real power lies in the powerlessness of the Cross; in the Bread of Life that is broken. When we cannot fight back, when we weep over our inadequacy, when our goodness is misunderstood, then, we will know the powerlessness of †Jesus. Then we will possess the same trust †Jesus had in the Father. Apostles of holiness, in their weakness, follow †Jesus. They love Him with all they are, and all they are not and yet to be; all that they fall short of accomplishing. They do not work for food that perishes, but for the food that endures to eternal life.

"†Jesus (said to Bartimaeus), 'Go your way; your faith has saved you.' Immediately he received his sight and followed him <u>on the way</u>" (Mark 10: 52).

"Lord †Jesus, how often I walk through life, eyes wide open, but seeing nothing. I do not see you in the helpless person, the needy person, the frightened person along the way who asks for my compassion and love. Too often, I think about only what is easy, what makes me happy or is in my best interest. Show me the way to throw off the layers that keep me from following you; from seeing you in your most distressing disguise. †Jesus, I want to see...so I can follow you – the Way, the Truth and the Life. So I can be a saint. Amen".

Faith, Failure and Trust

We are exploring FAITH and the call to holiness. We are exploring our faith in †Jesus, the One who suffered, died and rose on the third day; faith in †Jesus, who ascended into heaven and who sits at the right hand of the Father. But, we celebrate more than **our** faith in †Jesus. We celebrate the faith †Jesus has in us. We celebrate the fact that †Jesus entrusted His mission to His disciples who then handed this mission down through the centuries to us. Why in the world would †Jesus do this?

The Gospels relate the many failures of His first disciples. †Jesus directed them to cast their nets out into the deep water. They obeyed, but only to humor Him. They failed to believe. †Jesus told them to feed the 5000 with a few loaves and fish. His disciples complained that it was impossible. They failed to believe. Over and over again, they showed a complete lack of faith and trust in †Jesus. In the Garden of Gethsemane, in the moment of His greatest need, they abandoned Him; one betrayed Him, another denied Him and they all ran away. Despite ALL of this, †Jesus promised them:

"You will receive power when the Holy Spirit comes, and you will be my witnesses...to the ends of the earth" (Acts 1:8).

After all their failures †Jesus still believed in them. †Jesus entrusted to these men, the greatest endeavor in human

46

history. Was the faith of †Jesus in the Twelve mis-guided? NO! The "Good News" has been proclaimed to the ends of the earth. How did this happen amidst followers of such weakness? The power of the Holy Spirit is greater than any human failure. The presence of †Jesus in our life makes all things possible.

Faith in †Jesus is more than belief in the historical person from Nazareth. It is to trust His faith in us. Why do we fail to grow in the spiritual life? Because we don't believe we can be saints; we accept our human weakness as an incurable illness. We fail to believe in the power of Christ. †Jesus promises us that *"all things are possible"* if we believe in Him and His power at work in us.

In the Gospel, we have the words of †Jesus:

"These signs will accompany those who believe: in my name they will drive out demons, they will speak new languages, they will pick up serpents with their hands, and if they drink any deadly thing it will not harm them, they will lay hands on the sick, and they will recover" (Mark 16: 17-18).

I have personally experienced some of these things; not because I am a saint. For, you see, I am capable of really poor judgment and weakness. But, I won't give up on the power of †Jesus to work through me. Let me give you an example. A few years ago a woman and her husband came into my office. She was pregnant and they had just returned from her doctor who informed them that their unborn child would suffer from Down Syndrome. You can imagine how devastated they were at this news. We prayed together and I administered the Sacrament of the Anointing of the Sick to the mother. I told them to trust in God and assured them on my continued prayers for them and their unborn child. Within a year of their visit, another couple came to speak with me. The wife was pregnant with their first child and, again, the unborn child was diagnosed with Down Syndrome. This young couple was equally devastated as the first couple was. I anointed this mother; we all prayed together and promised to remain in prayer throughout the pregnancy and trust in God. Both babies were born healthy. I witnessed firsthand the power of the Sacrament of the Anointing of the Sick. I am sure the surprised doctors excused this as a misdiagnosis. But we know it was a miracle. These are the signs †Jesus spoke of that would come to those who believe.

Even in the midst of failure †Jesus has never given up on me. †Jesus continues to entrust me with His mission as His priest. †Jesus has faith in every one of you! He has poured out His Spirit upon you. If you believe His faith in you is misplaced, you will never advance in the spiritual life; you will never be a saint. You must stop focusing on failure and weakness and set your gaze on †Jesus: His love, His power, His trust in you.

The Gospel passage concludes: *"The disciples went forth and the Lord worked with them"* (Mark 16:20). †Jesus will work with you. Look what He did with a few loaves and fish! Never think you are on this mission alone. In his book, The Cenacle, Bishop Giaquinta writes:

"Christ will always be present through His generative Church. From Christ's pierced side flow water and blood as the Fathers of the Church have commented: Baptism and Eucharist, the two sacraments that generate the Church...After the Ascension Christ disappears visibly from history's scene since the Apostles will make Him sacramentally present from now on. Likewise, after the Apostles give witness with their own blood, their successors will continue Christ's generative presence through time". [xiv]

Each one of us shares in the apostolic ministry through the priesthood handed down from those first followers of †Jesus. Some are called to the ordained priesthood; all are called to the common priesthood of the faithful. Each one of us is given a mission by †Jesus. Maybe you don't want it. Maybe you think what He asks is too difficult or simply impossible. Be courageous and face your mission, your vocation, with trust. Believe that †Jesus has given you the grace to succeed.

"That you may know...the surpassing greatness of His power for us who believe" (Ephesians 1:18-19).

You must show †Jesus that His faith in you is well-founded. †Jesus will not give up on you. He has faith in you. †Jesus will work with you. Believe that *"all things are possible with God"*. Do not give up on †Jesus. Believe in His faith in you.

2. HOPE

There Is Hope For Everyone

O Lord God,
I hope by your grace for the
pardon of all my sins
and after life here to gain
eternal   happiness
because you have promised it
who are infinitely powerful,
faithful, kind, and merciful.
In this hope I intend to live and
die.
Amen.

.

When we celebrate the feast of the Assumption of Mary into Heaven, the words of Mary's Magnificat express a joy-filled Mary.

> *"My soul proclaims the greatness of the Lord;*
> *my spirit rejoices in God my savior.*

For he has looked upon his handmaid's lowliness;
behold, from now on will all ages call me blessed"
(Luke 1:46-48).

What is the source of Mary's joy? She carries within her, the hope of the world - †Jesus, the Savior of the world. John, who is growing in the womb of Elizabeth, would be *"a voice of one crying out in the desert, prepare the way of the Lord"* (Matthew 3:3). His would be a message of joy: the Christ, the long-awaited Messiah, is coming. What is the cause of all this joy going around in ancient Judea? It is HOPE. It is the expectation of a new life and a new beginning.

"He has sent me to bring glad tidings to the lowly, to heal the broken-hearted, to proclaim liberty to the captives, and release to prisoners" (Isaiah 61:1).

This is all accomplished through †Jesus. Bishop Giaquinta writes:

"Why, then, did Christ, instead of choosing the minimum to redeem us, choose the maximum? He did it to make us aware of the seriousness of sin, but most of all because he wanted to show us the immensity of His love as we read in John's (Gospel): 'There is no greater love than this, to lay down one's life for one's friends' (John 15:13). And so Christ, to show His infinite love for us, dies on the Cross". [xv]

Our joy comes from our hope in Christ and His infinite love for us.

The traditional Christian symbol of hope is the anchor: that saving instrument on ships when tossed around by winds and waves on stormy seas. The anchor keeps the ship stable. We are tossed by the winds and the waves of life. We are looking for some stability in the chaos. The virtue of hope brings that stability. Hope in a bright future carries a student through the drudgery of classes and exams. Hope of a blissful life carries a young couple to the altar for marriage. Hope in emerging beauty enables an artist to face an empty canvas. Hope that a utopia of saints is possible encouraged Bishop Giaquinta to form the Pro Sanctity Movement and the various Institutes affiliated with the Movement. The hope that one can make a difference in the world draws a person to the ordained or consecrated life.

But human hope is fragile. There is a gap that exists between what we have and what we hope for. There is a distance between the present and the future. No power on earth can remove that waiting. Human hope carries with it the element of uncertainty. This is not the case with Divine Hope. There is no gap between present and future. †Jesus declared: *"The Kingdom of God is at hand"*. The source of our hope is that God is with us – NOW! In a homily from 2006, Pope Benedict XVI reflected:

"The hope which is in Christ is in the world, is for the world, but it is precisely because Christ is God, is 'the

Holy One'. Christ is hope for the world because He is risen". [xvi]

God can intervene in our lives, NOW, if we let Him. Yet, we are often turned in on self. There is no room for God. Recall Michelangelo's <u>Last Judgment</u>, painted on the wall of the Sistine Chapel. A figure just below †Jesus and to the left epitomizes the one without hope; curled up and turned in on them self. No situation in life is hopeless. If only we turn to God. And maybe the result might not be what we expected. We must never forget that, *"God's ways are not our ways"*.

If joy has been elusive in your life perhaps you are seeking solutions in all the wrong places. Do we look for worldly, secular answers to the questions in our life? They will never satisfy us for long. Joy comes from placing our hope in †Jesus. In the solutions He proposes: love, self-gift, patience, kindness, compassion and forgiveness.

"Serenity, gladness and joy must be the first factors that attract people (to us). This joy and serenity, however, must not be merely external, but the outpouring of deep, inner sentiments stemming from our vocation". [xvii]

The joy that is the outpouring of hope is rooted in this conviction: that we are called to holiness; that sanctity is within our reach. Sanctity is lived out, practically, in the life †Jesus proposed in the Sermon on the Mount and the Beatitudes:

"Blessed are the poor in spirit; for theirs is the Kingdom of Heaven.

Blessed are they who mourn; for they will be comforted.

Blessed are the meek; for they will inherit the land.

Blessed are they who hunger and thirst for righteousness; for they will be satisfied.

Blessed are the merciful; for they will be shown mercy.

Blessed are the clean of heart; for they will see God.

Blessed are the peacemakers; for they will be called children of God.

Blessed are they who are persecuted for the sake of righteousness; for theirs is the Kingdom of Heaven" (Matt 5: 3-10).

Joy emerges from the virtuous life. Joy emerges from the deep, inner virtue of hope. There may be no immediate gratification since this is what our secular culture offers. We must remember that worldly pleasure is only temporary and fleeting. Hope in †Jesus brings lasting results; a joy that is not fleeting; an anchor that keeps us safe in stormy seas.

St. Luke gives us a glimpse into the personality of a Man of Hope: John the Baptist. It may seem strange to think of John as a man of hope. We more readily see him as someone who preached doom and gloom. The Prophet Isaiah described John as:

"A voice of one crying out in the desert: 'Prepare the way of the Lord', make straight his paths" (Luke 3:4).

Yet, at the same time, John gave hope to the people who came to the Jordan to be baptized:

"Every valley shall be filled and every mountain and hill shall be made low. The winding roads shall be made straight, and the rough ways shall be made smooth, and all flesh shall see the salvation of God" (Luke 3: 5-6).

John spoke openly. He was not afraid to speak the truth. His message was not doom and gloom. It was a message of HOPE. Notice how John has a hopeful word for each group that approached him. The tax collectors were shunned by fellow Jews. They were considered collaborators with the Romans as well as crooks – collecting more in taxes than what was required. John instructed them to be just and honest. They, too, could enjoy the salvation promised by Yahweh. Notice how the soldiers were given hope. They were Romans and Gentiles. They were hated by Jews. John even had words of hope for them. The Lord would welcome them, too. But, they must live with integrity and not be cruel. This must have instilled joy in their hearts. A joy that comes from the hope they must have felt; the hope that <u>no</u> <u>one</u> is lost. †Jesus came to save all people. He is the One Savior of the world: yesterday, today and forever. St. Paul describes the reason for our joy:

"Rejoice in the Lord always. I shall say it again: Rejoice... the Lord is near" (Colossians 4: 4-5).

†Jesus is near. He is: Emmanuel: *"God is with us"*.

"The Lord has removed the judgment against you...The King of Israel, the Lord, is in your midst, you have no further misfortune to fear" (Zephaniah 3: 15).

Do we believe this? Do we believe that God is close to us? Those who do not believe this lack hope.

Who is the person of Hope? The one who overcomes discouragement; who understands that today's trials are temporary; the person that recognizes *"God is with us"*. St. Paul encourages us with words like this:

"If God is for us who can be against us? He who did not spare His own Son but handed Him over for us all, how will he also not give us everything else along with Him" (Romans 8: 31-32).

The person of hope is a person of joy. St. Paul describes the joyful person:

"Your kindness should be known to all" (Colossians 4:5).

The person of hope is a joyful giver. They never count the cost of an act of love or kindness. They know they will never be diminished by their generosity. Because the one who baptizes with the Holy Spirit and fire will always provide for them. They are joyful in giving because their faith is strong and their hope is unflinching.

This is the kind of person John the Baptist was. He lacked material comforts. He wore camel hair for clothing; he feasted on locusts and wild honey. He had very little. But his message was full of hope. A message he was willing to share with everyone: tax collectors, Gentiles, the occupying Roman army, those rejected by society. Even to those who would reject him. †Gentle God would complete what was lacking in his ministry. John was an extraordinarily successful preacher. He was a man steeped in humility, generosity and passion. His life, however, ended prematurely. When he could give God nothing more - he would give his life. John was a man of hope because he emptied himself, of self. This he did so he could be filled with the Lord; the Lord who was near. John always knew the Lord was near. From the first moment he leaped for joy in his mother's womb when Mary came to visit.

John's message, the message of the Gospel, is this: no person is hopeless. This truth keeps me, as a priest and confessor, encouraged as I celebrate the Sacrament of Reconciliation with the faithful. St. Paul writes:

"May the God of peace Himself make you perfectly holy and may you entirely, spirit, soul, and body, be preserved blameless for the coming of our Lord †Jesus Christ. The One who calls you is faithful, and he will accomplish it" (1 Thessalonians 5: 23-24).

The Apostle to the Gentiles is telling us that God will never give up on us. He will help us to be holy. We should not give up on ourselves or others.

The Sacred Scriptures are very clear. **There is hope for everyone!** Regardless of how we have messed up our relationship with God: **There is hope for everyone!** This is not some new interpretation of the Word of God. It is a truth as old as salvation history. In the Second Book of Chronicles: *"The leaders, priests and people added infidelity to infidelity"* (2 Chronicles 36: 14). The Israelite people repeatedly disobeyed God. It was almost a way of life for them. But, *"Early and often did the Lord, the God of their fathers have compassion on His people"* (2 Chronicles 36:15). God would not turn His back on them. Why? Because, **there is hope for everyone!**

The Israelite's disobedience caused them to be defeated and held captive in Babylon for 70 years. The Lord then inspired King Cyrus to free His people. Why? Because, **there is hope for everyone!** Why is there hope for everyone; even the most hard-hearted? St. Paul writes: *"God is rich in mercy"* (Ephesians 2: 4) (*"Dives in Misericordia"*). When God's people were spiritually dead God brought them to life through the sacrifice of Christ. What did we do to deserve God's mercy? St. Paul responds: Nothing! It is not the result of our efforts: *"By grace you have been saved"* (Ephesians 2: 15). In John's Gospel, †Jesus explains this to Nicodemus,

"God so loved the world, that he gave His only Son...that we might not perish, but have eternal life" (John 3:16).

This is the sign we see behind goal posts and basketball hoops. Always remember when you see written on a sign, John 3:16: **There is hope for everyone!**

Every Good Friday, we recall how †Jesus suffered and died for us. He did this because He knew there is hope for me and you. After the Resurrection †Jesus walked along the Sea of Galilee with Peter (John 21: 15-19). This is the same apostle who denied Him three times. Yet, three times †Jesus told Peter: *"Feed my sheep"*. Why would †Jesus entrust leadership to Peter? Because, **there is hope for everyone!**

In the Lord's Prayer, we pray: *"Forgive us our trespasses as we forgive those who trespass against us"*. Why must I forgive that person who hurt me? That person who betrayed me? Because, **there is hope for everyone!** †Jesus does not give up on us because He looks beyond our sin. He sees our potential; what we can become. †Jesus knows we can become saints! †Jesus has great hope in us. We should not give up on ourselves, either. We should not settle for a life of weakness and selfishness simply because we keep making the same mistakes. †Jesus will not give up on us. Why? Because, **there is hope for everyone!** It is this truth that keeps me striving to be holy; striving to be a saint. Never give up on your call to holiness.

When you die and go to heaven, you will see people you never thought would be there. You will <u>then</u> know: **there is hope for everyone!** Hope is THE Christian virtue. It separates believers from non-believers. Atheists can have faith in something; they are capable of heroic love. But, they do not have hope. The call to holiness demands that I be a person of hope; a person rich in mercy. Early and often, I must show compassion. †Jesus says, **there is hope for everyone!** Why?

"God so loved the world, that he gave His only Son...that we might not perish, but have eternal life" (John 3:16)

Over fifty years ago, The Second Vatican Council published the document: <u>The Church in the Modern World</u>. It is often known by its Latin title: <u>Gaudium et Spes</u>. This title means: <u>Joy and Hope</u>. This is how we must face the modern world. Not in cynicism, bitterness, jealousy or selfishness. We must face our world with joy and hope. We must live with hope even in difficult times. Only then, can we come to know the joy of Christ. It is chapter five of the Second Vatican Council document, <u>Lumen Gentium</u>, which is of particular interest to us.   The chapter is entitled: "The Universal Call to Holiness".

"All Christians in any state or walk in life are called to the fullness of the Christian life and to the perfection of love, and by this holiness a more human manner of life is fostered also in society". [xviii]

The document reads "All Christians". **There is hope for everyone!** Through a life of hope we will receive what †Jesus promised His disciples at the Last Supper.

"My joy will be in you and your joy will be complete" (John 15: 11).

Mary: Woman Of Hope

*O Mary, you are immaculate and completely
holy; what would the world have received
from you if not Him who would be born holy?
The Spirit of God, overshadowing you
with its mysterious presence, begot him
in your immaculate womb.
In humility you gave birth to him who was
God but became man for our salvation
and for the sanctification of the world.
You are Mother.
Mother of all those who bear witness with
their blood and thus heroically prove their
love for your Son; Mother also of those
who bear witness to their love with the
holiness of their lives. Mother of us all.
You who are now in heaven, continue your
work as a mediatrix of sanctification among
us who live on earth.
Grant us love for your Son, the joy of the
Spirit, the Father's craving for perfection,
and the hope of joining you in the land of
the saints. Amen.*

(+G. Giaquinta)

Hope is the bridge between Faith and Love. Hope deepens by listening to God's word. There are three virtues necessary for listening: courage, compassion and charity.

We must have courage to <u>follow</u> †Jesus. To be a disciple, I must have the courage to <u>listen</u> to †Jesus; to live the <u>truth</u> taught by †Jesus; to live in a <u>way</u> that our culture ridicules. The greatest obstacle to listening is fear. We ask, *'What are people going to say?' 'Am I going to miss out on something?'* Following †Jesus will often lead to what is unknown and uncomfortable. Most people prefer to do things the easy way; follow the path of least resistance. Because of this we hesitate in listening to †Jesus. But the Lord says through His prophet:

"Say to those whose hearts are frightened: Be strong, fear not...then the ears of the deaf will be cleared" (Isaiah 35:4-5).

In the Gospel of Mark we read a miracle story that is more than a cure. The story teaches a deeper reality.

"And people brought to (†Jesus) a deaf man who had a speech impediment and begged him to lay his hand on him. He took him off by himself away from the crowd. He put his finger into the man's ears and, spitting, touched his tongue; then he looked up to heaven and groaned, and said to him, "Ephphatha!" (that is, "Be opened!") And (immediately) the man's ears were opened, his speech impediment was removed, and he spoke plainly" (Mark 7: 32-36).

Here, we find †Jesus in Gentile territory. He walks among non-Jews and non-believers. The deaf man represents those without faith; those who do not listen to †Jesus. Do we ever wonder why our faith, hope and love are so slow to mature? It is generally because we are deaf to the words of †Jesus. If the Word of God or the teaching of the Magisterium is no more important than <u>People</u> magazine or supermarket tabloids, we will never growspiritually. It was only after the deaf man began to hear that he was filled with hope, proclaiming his faith in †Jesus.

When I listen with courage, I listen with hope. I am able to trust that †Jesus is with me; to help me. I am able to evangelize with boldness, with confidence. Saint John Paul II reminded us:

"To evangelize is the grace and vocation proper to the Church, her most profound identity...I urgently desire to encourage all the ministers of God's people, particularly those living in America, to take up this project and to cooperate in carrying it out. In accepting this mission, everyone should keep in mind that the vital core of the new evangelization must be a clear and unequivocal proclamation of the person of †Jesus Christ, that is, the preaching of His name, His teaching, His life, His promises, and the Kingdom which He has gained for us by His Paschal Mystery". [xix]

Mary listened with hope rather than fear. This is why she is *"blessed among women"*. The Magnificat is a prayer of hope:

"He has looked with favor on His lowly servant...He has shown might with His arms, dispersed the arrogant of mind and heart...He has thrown down the rulers from their thrones but lifted up the lowly. The hungry He has filled with good things; the rich He has sent away empty. He has helped Israel His servant, remembering His mercy, according to His promise to our fathers, to Abraham and His children forever" (cf: Luke 1: 46-53).

As a Magnificat people, we must place our hope in the promises God has made throughout salvation history.

Listening also demands the virtue of <u>COMPASSION.</u> Compassion is listening with the HEART. The heart is the place where I make my fundamental option for or against God; where I choose to listen or not. It is the place of authentic prayer. Prayer is the pathway to living out the apostolate of holiness.

"The life of perfection has two phases. Initially, the soul starts from nothingness and reaches the giving of the ALL she possesses to others. It starts from penance and reaches the apostolate through contemplation, through love". ˣˣ

Love is the manifestation of a heart that listens with compassion. I am able to *"suffer with"* those I serve in the apostolate. To love to the maximum, with ALL my heart, ALL my soul, ALL my strength and ALL my mind, is manifested in the mature, hope-filled disciple. †Jesus would remind us: *"where your heart is, there is your treasure"*. As with prayer, listening is superficial if it does not penetrate the depths of the heart. The virtue of compassion is expressed when I listen from my heart; I am able to see the suffering †Jesus in other people. I am able to respond to the Lord's call to help them. It is an expression of a hope-filled heart. My compassion expresses to the world that I listen to †Jesus. I hold on to every word He proclaims.

Without the virtue of CHARITY, I am deaf as a stone. This is the third virtue necessary for listening.

"Beloved, let us love one another, because love is of God; everyone who loves is begotten of God and knows God...for God is love" (1 John 4:7-8).

The Holy Spirit will always direct us to acts of charity. Selfishness shows that I care more about myself than I do about God or others; that I am deaf to the voice of †Jesus. †Jesus calls us to the perfection of love – holiness. What is the sign that I am truly listening to †Jesus? How my life is expressed on the level of <u>love</u>. All the prayer in the world means nothing, if I am not living a life manifested by love. Without the virtue of hope, love is self-serving. I care only about what pleases me. The promises of †Jesus are irrelevant. Or worse, I take them for granted. I believe I can do what I want and still enjoy eternal life. Without hope, love will never lead me to union with God. It cannot lead me to holiness. Returning to the Gospel story, we read that the deaf man had a speech impediment. The Greek word used here means *'he could not speak coherently'*. His words were confusing. Only after †Jesus cured his <u>deafness</u> could he then be understood by others. Once he could listen <u>clearly</u> there was no confusing speech.

Our lives can be a jumble of mixed loyalties and feelings; confusing to others and ourselves. At times, we seem to blow with every wind. St. Paul also struggled with confusing loyalties.

"For I do not do what I want to do, but I do what I hate...For I take delight in the law of God, in my inner self, but I see in my members another principle at war with the law of my mind, taking me captive to the law of sin that dwells in my members" (Romans 7: 15, 22-23).

It is only when we start listening to God's voice that our lives will be less confusing; that we will have real direction, real clarity. The Apostle Thomas, confused, asked †Jesus:

"'Master, we don't know where you are going; how can we know the way?' †Jesus said to him: 'I am the Way, the Truth and the Life. No one comes to the Father except through me'" (John 14: 5-6).

Isn't this what we all want? We desire real direction, leading us to the Lord? But first, we must learn to listen to †Jesus. We must learn to discipline ourselves to recognize His voice; to turn a deaf ear to the counter-spirit, our human selfishness, to the voices of our culture. †Jesus will show us the way. We must allow †Jesus to cure the deafness that is caused by the noisy din of the world. Bishop Giaquinta once said:

"Our involvement in society through our work does not justify focusing our attention on everything that interests us or following our own tastes. What we have is not ours but belongs to the Church". [xxi]

Bishop Giaquinta echoes a reality that even a great mystic, like St. Teresa of Avila, struggled with in her life.

"I was living an extremely burdensome life, because in prayer I understood more clearly my faults. On the one hand God was calling me; on the other hand I was following the world. All the things of God made me happy; those of the world held me bound. It seems I desired to harmonize these two contraries... such as are the spiritual life and sensory joys, pleasures, and pastimes. In prayer I was having great trouble, for my spirit was not proceeding as lord but as slave. And so I was not able to shut myself within myself (which was my whole manner of procedure in prayer); instead, I shut myself within a thousand vanities". [xxii]

To place our hope in God, keeps our heart centered on what is important. My life is hope-filled when I listen to God's Word: in Sacred Scripture, in the teachings of the Church, in prayer and recollection. This demands that we listen with Courage, Compassion and Charity. Not caring what others might think or say. But, rather, by caring for the suffering Christ we see in those who are in need; by living with the desire to be holy as God is holy. Then, from lives of confusion and desperation comes hope. And from hope will spring forth, "living water".

We can look to Mary as a woman of Hope. Mary is a model of listening to God in Prayer. At the Annunciation, the Angel Gabriel asked Mary to become the mother of God. With her *"yes"*, her *"fiat"*, †Jesus was conceived by the power of the Holy Spirit. His human life began at conception. Thirty three years later, His life would end on Calvary. There was one witness to both events: Mary – the mother of †Jesus. From the birth of †Jesus to his death, Mary's heart would be pierced by a sword. Mary was fully united with her son's passion. Yet she never fell into despair. She never stopped trusting God. She was filled with hope in His promises. Mary is the faithful *"handmaid of the Lord"*. She is the mystical rose of Yahweh.

Mary teaches us how to embrace the mystical life amid the tragedies and triumphs of daily life. Mary teaches us the way of docility to the Spirit. Again, I refer to the statement of Fr. Karl Rahner, S.J.: "The Christian of the future will be a mystic, or not exist at all". Mary is the model of the Christian mystic. She is an example of the patient, hope-filled disciple, who does not fully understand God's plan. But, she allows that plan to unfold day after day.

Sacred Scripture reveals that Mary *"pondered"* events in her heart. To *"ponder"* is <u>not</u> an intellectual exercise; as if trying to find the answer to a question;

looking for a solution to a problem. To *"ponder"* is to patiently hold something inside my soul. Even with all the tension involved: the tension of not understanding; the tension of not knowing the reason; the tension of pure faith and hope. Mary stood beneath the Cross and watched †Jesus die. There was nothing she can do to save her Son. She could not even protest His innocence and goodness. No one would listen to her. The crowd simply jeered and ridiculed her Son as He hung from the cross. Mary is *"pondering"* in the biblical sense. Mary carries within her a great tension: that she is helpless to resolve His suffering; that she must live with the death of her Son. This is what Scripture refers to when it tells us that Mary *"kept these things in her heart and pondered them"* (Luke 2: 19).

For all of us, to "ponder" in the biblical sense is to stand before life's great mysteries just as Mary stood before the various mysteries of the life of †Jesus. Including the way she stood before the Cross. It is not to be bitter or blaming. It is to accept the unknowable, the unreasonable and the unanswerable. It is to accept, that life is not always fair. To *"ponder"* is to carry the great questions of life as Mary did. It is to have hope in God's power: His power to help us overcome what we think is impossible to overcome. It is to embrace a hope that opens the door to spiritual joy in the midst of suffering. Here is a mysticism that revitalizes our lost hope; only if we are willing to *"ponder"* in the biblical sense; to trust and hope in God, rather than bitterly, angrily, questioning His will. Instead of crying out: *"Why me, Lord"?* we pray: *"Why am I so loved?"* It is easy to embrace the triumphs of life. But, the mystic emerges from the Crosses of life; by how we *"ponder"* the Cross of Christ; by how we stand before life's great mysteries. Bishop Giaquinta writes:

"The Lord is a great artist, and He Himself, will give us ways to make our soul pliable. Be careful never to say 'no' to Him but to answer always with the 'Fiat' of the Blessed Virgin Mary: 'Be it done to me according to your word' (Luke 1:38). In sorrow and in sadness, in sickness and in humiliations, in poverty and in need, in dryness and in lack of understanding, 'Fiat', always 'Fiat'". [xxiii]

The mystic prays unceasingly. The mystic prays through all life's events looking for the presence of God; rejoicing in the good or just simply trying to hold on, especially in challenging times. It is the virtue of hope that allows us to *"ponder"* and to carry the tensions of life. Pondering as Mary did, from the Annunciation to the Crucifixion, will deepen our faith, hope and love: The greatest virtues; the three things that last. To *"ponder"* in the biblical sense, is the way of †Jesus who...

"emptied Himself...becoming obedient to the point of death, even death on a cross" (Philippians 2: 7-8).

It is the way of the Christian mystic.

"Be doers of the word and not hearers only, deluding yourselves. For if anyone is a hearer of the word and not a doer, he is like a man who looks at his own face in a mirror. He sees himself, then he goes off and promptly forgets what he looked like. But the one who peers into the perfect law of freedom and perseveres, and is not a hearer who forgets but a doer who acts, such a one shall be blessed in what he does" (James 1:22-25).

The Letter of James describes the movement from the Old Testament description of the Mosaic Law to the Gospel of †Jesus Christ that brings freedom. Here we have the image of the person who hears God's word. This is the person who truly <u>listens</u> in the heart; the person who has become one with the Word of God. The Word of God is an integral part of their life. To *"ponder"*, as Mary did, is to <u>listen</u> in the depths of my being. It is not to dismiss what I read or hear as irrelevant, whether it is from the Sacred Scriptures or the teaching authority of the Church. It is to recognize the presence of God in what I hear or experience.

"Know this, my dear (ones), everyone should be quick to hear, slow to speak, slow to wrath...humbly welcome the word that has been planted in you and is able to save your soul" (James 1: 19, 21).

We can obey the will of God in one of two ways: with DOCILITY or with RESIGNATION. Docility is to obey God with hope and trust, confident that all will be well. Resignation is to obey God with a disposition of suspicion:

I am not sure that I can trust God. I obey Him grudgingly. We see both forms of listening expressed in the first chapter of Luke's Gospel.

First is the story of Zachariah. The father of John was resigned to God's will following the news about his wife's upcoming pregnancy. Next, we hear the story of the Annunciation. Mary was actively receptive to the word given her by the angel. She listened and accepted God's plan for her. She listened with joy and with docility.

The questions we ask ourselves are: How do I listen to God: with docility or with resignation? As Mary did or as Zachariah did? Do I listen with active receptivity or argumentatively? One will result in peace. The other will result in anxiety. At the heart of docility is what the angel declared to Mary in his last words to her.

"Nothing will be impossible for God" (Luke 1:37).

All things can be overcome with God's grace; every hardship, tragedy and challenge. This belief should move us to listen to God and accept His will with docility. This is the truest expression of our hope in His promises. We are to readily accept the Gospel and act in conformity with the Good News. We are to remove from our soul whatever is opposed to the Gospel. By *"pondering"* we are able to explore the real depth and meaning of God's Word in our life. The Word of God becomes planted in us so that it may take root and lead us to holiness. This is how the mystic listens.

To listen to the Gospel and not practice it results in a failure to improve oneself; a failure to respond to God's invitation to be a saint. Only when I conform my life to the perfect law of freedom, can I receive the joy promised by †Jesus:

"That my joy may be in you and your joy might be complete" (John 15:11).

This is how listening becomes prayer, and prayer becomes pondering, and pondering leads to the perfection of love. This is how the Christian mystic responds to the Universal Call to Holiness: making the journey from Calvary to the empty tomb. This is the way that hope replaces fear, bridging the gap between faith and love, leading us to the perfection of love – holiness. It is in a hope-filled *"pondering"* that we carry Christ with us, every moment of our life.

"Christ continues to suffer throughout the centuries. He continues His life and work of redemption on earth no longer through a personal, interior anguish, but through the outward sacrifice and immolation of His Body. Once He suffered in His physical body, today He continues to suffer in His mystical Body. Therefore, we, the members of this Body, must feel the duty and responsibility to participate in the unceasing agony and Passion that †Jesus continues to live through us, throughout the centuries". [xxiv]

The call to holiness is the vocation to *"ponder"* the crosses of life. It is to carry life's tensions within, rather than running away from them. When we are able to do this, Hope, for the Apostle of Holiness, is the anchor amidst the stormy seas.

Daring To Trust

Mary remains one of the most enduring figures in Christianity. From paintings by the great masters, to the Nativity scene in your home, Mary is venerated as the Mother of God. We often imagine her as a pious, meek, woman surrounded in a heavenly haze or living in unapproachable light. But this image is unrealistic. In reality, Mary was very human. She was without sin but lived a deeply human life; a difficult and challenging life. To truly appreciate and understand Mary's holiness we must understand her humanity. Combining theology and history we get a more realistic image of Mary.

Mary was probably called "Miriam", after the sister of Moses. Mary spoke Aramaic with a Galilean accent. She, likely, belonged to the peasant class trying to make a living through farming and small trades. Joseph and †Jesus were not part of a lucrative profession. Carpentry was not a well-paying trade. The social group they belonged to made up 90% of the population. They bore the burden of supporting the state and the small privileged class. Their life was very difficult. Imposed on them was a triple tax burden: Rome, Herod, and the temple tax of 10%. To have a steady supply of food, carpentry was combined with farming. Carpenters of the time were often stone-cutters. Wood was not readily available and stone was plentiful. This might be where

†Jesus became so familiar with *"cornerstones"* and *"stones rejected by the builder"*. Even today, in Israel, buildings are predominantly stone. It is more than likely Mary worked as a field laborer to supplement the family income.

It is unlikely the Holy Family lived in a quiet, quaint home with a carpenter's workshop in the rear, or even attached to it. As was the custom of the time, they probably lived with an extended family: three or four small cottages of one or two rooms around an open courtyard. They may have lived with relatives and shared an oven, a cistern and a millstone for grinding. Mary likely spent ten or more hours a day on domestic chores: carrying water from a well or cistern, gathering wood for the fire, cooking meals, cleaning the cottage and washing clothes. Mary was not unlike many hard-working women today.

It would be a mistake to think of Mary as a fragile woman. She was capable of walking the hill country of Judea, while pregnant, giving birth to her son in a cave, making the four or five day journey on foot to Jerusalem once a year and sleeping in open country with other pilgrims. Mary engaged in hard labor, daily. Mary probably had a robust physique, not the beautifully dressed, golden-haired Madonna who adorns our Christmas cards.

It is doubtful Mary knew how to read. Literacy was rare among women of her time. The culture was highly oral and public reading of the Hebrew Scriptures was common. Traditions were passed down through the telling of stories. Mary most likely told the stories of the birth of †Jesus and His childhood to others and these stories were passed down to the evangelists.

Mary was widowed before the public ministry of †Jesus. At the time of His crucifixion she was at least 50 years old, beyond the age when most women of her time had died. It is likely she outlived most of her friends and family. Mary lived into the early years of the Church telling stories of their family life and giving comfort and support to the early Christian community.

Why is it important to know the historical Mary? This knowledge brings Mary closer to us. She is more like billions of people today than the woman we gaze at in beautiful art. She had a difficult life, struggling to make ends meet.

Her holiness lies in her persistent, faith-filled listening to God – in her prayer. She persevered faithfully in everyday life. Mary had to figure out what God was asking of her; looking for His word in people and events and taking those experiences to prayer. Bishop Giaquinta reminds us of the importance of prayer:

"Through prayer, miracles can be obtained – not necessarily physical miracles, but miracles that touch our life, our spirit. We must try to accomplish these miracles in our life following the example of Mary, our Blessed Mother, her life of prayer and contemplation". [xxv]

Mary pondered God's Word in her heart and acted on that Word. Day by day, she lived a pilgrimage of faith. Despite the many hardships and tragedies of life, she responded: *"Let it be done to me as you say"*.

Mary's Magnificat is our song of freedom; the song of those who live in surrender to God. Mary epitomizes the lowly of Israel for whom there is *"no room at the Inn"*. Despite her many hardships Mary always sings the praises of God.

Why is Mary important in the life of the Church? Giuliana Spigione, former Major Sister of the Institute of Apostolic Oblates, expressed it this way in 2006 before her death:

"Ahead of us is Mary who teaches us to walk, Mary, the Confidence that shows us the Child as she showed Him to the shepherds. We also, with joy in our hearts, must announce Him to the world. We must carry Him into the heart of the world. Perhaps we must ask if today we are the 'apostles' who know how to communicate to the world the joy of the encounter with God?" [xxvi]

Mary believed God could turn the world upside down: the last can be first, the humble are exalted, those that lose their life will save it and those who mourn, will someday rejoice.

We often believe there is a limit to what we can do. Bishop Guiquinta believed differently:

"Sometimes we tend to believe that there is a limit to the spiritual life – a limit that cannot be overcome. We know

82

that there is no limit to conversion...Before God we know that our nature, our inclinations tend more toward what is negative...Therefore, we need to overcome our nature, to correct our inclinations; sometimes it is necessary to do violence to our nature".

What kind of violence? Bishop Giaquinta declares: "†Jesus Himself said: 'You must deny yourselves...take up your cross...'" [xxvii]

The historical Mary experienced poverty, oppression, violence and the execution of her Son. She was not among the world's powerful; she was simply God's maidservant. She believed *"Nothing is impossible with God"*. The Magnificat has nothing of the sweet nostalgic tones of Christmas carols. It is a song about collapsing thrones and humbled Lords; about the power of God and the powerlessness of humanity.

Mary is *"Blessed among women"* not because she was privileged but because she trusted God through everyday hardship. Mary <u>dared</u> to trust God. It is why we call her: "Our Mother of Trust". Pope Benedict XVI, in a homily of December 8th 2006, invites us to imagine Mary speaking these words to us:

"Have the courage to dare with God! Try it! Do not be afraid of Him! Have the courage to risk with faith! Have the courage to risk with goodness! Have the courage to risk with a pure heart! Commit yourselves to God, then you will see, that it is precisely by doing so, that your life will become broad and light, not boring, but filled with infinite surprises, for God's goodness is never depleted."

Mary lived with much less than we do. She had only one star over the stable yet, daily, we can count our lucky stars. She dared to say "yes" to God. She dared to give herself totally to God. According to Bishop Giaquinta, this is at the heart of the Apostolate of Holiness:

"Apostolate is: being totally given. That is, totally given for what we are and in what we have. This, for me, is apostolate and it can be carried out everywhere, whether we are working in a kitchen, on a job, etc. The important thing is to be totally given" [xxviii] (Retreat; 21 July 1982).

Mary, the Mother of God, was a woman totally given; a model for the apostolate of holiness: *"Blessed among women"*.

Draw Near To †Jesus

Tax collectors and sinners were all drawing near to listen to †Jesus, but the Pharisees and scribes began to complain, saying, "This man welcomes sinners and eats with them." So to them †Jesus addressed this parable: "A man had two sons, and the younger son said to his father, 'Father, give me the share of your estate that should come to me.' So the father divided the property between them. After a few days, the younger son collected all his belongings and set off to a distant country where he squandered his inheritance on a life of dissipation. When he had freely spent everything, a severe famine struck that country, and he found himself in dire need. So he hired himself out to one of the local citizens who sent him to his farm to tend the swine. And he longed to eat his fill of the pods on which the swine fed, but nobody gave him any. Coming to his senses he thought, 'How many of my father's hired workers have more than enough food to eat, but here am I, dying from hunger. I shall get up and go to my father and I shall say to him, "Father, I have sinned against heaven and against you. I no longer deserve to be called your son; treat me as you would treat one of your hired workers."' So he got up and went back to his father. While he was still a long way off, his father caught sight of him, and was filled with compassion. He ran to his son, embraced him and kissed him. His son said to him, 'Father, I have sinned against heaven and against you; I no longer deserve to be called your son.' But his father ordered his servants, 'Quickly bring the finest robe and put it on him; put a ring on his finger and sandals on his feet. Take the fattened calf and slaughter it. Then let us celebrate with a feast, because this son of mine was dead, and has come to life again; he was lost, and has been found.' Then the celebration began. Now the older son had been out in the field and, on his way back, as he neared the house, he heard the sound of music and dancing. He called one of the servants and asked what this might mean. The servant said to him, 'Your brother has returned and your father has slaughtered the fattened calf because he has him back safe and sound.' He became angry, and when he refused to enter the house, his father came out and pleaded with him. He said to his father in reply, 'Look, all these years I served you and not once did I disobey your orders; yet you never gave me even a young goat to feast on with my friends. But when your son returns who swallowed up your property with prostitutes, for him you slaughter the fattened calf.' He said to him, 'My son, you are here with me always; everything I have is yours. But now we must celebrate and rejoice, because your brother was dead and has come to life again; he was lost and has been found.'"

Lk 15:1-3, 11-32

How close are you to †Jesus? Do you feel a deep intimacy with the Lord? Your faith tells you that He is near you. Well...maybe you at least HOPE He is near. In all honesty, you just don't know, for sure. Maybe you don't feel very close to †Jesus. We all wish we felt closer. We all wish we <u>were</u> closer. But, in reality, †Jesus is often a distant acquaintance. We don't think of Him that often. At Mass we do, when we are not distracted. We think of Him when we are in trouble and when we need something. What is blocking us from a close relationship with †Jesus? There can be many things. The Gospel reveals at least one of those barriers: unremitted sin.

"Tax Collectors and sinners were all <u>drawing</u> <u>near</u> to †Jesus".

How could <u>they</u> *"draw near"* to †Jesus and we struggle so much? This verse refers to more than physical proximity to †Jesus. It also means they were drawing spiritually close to †Jesus. They had opened their hearts to the words of †Jesus. They recognized that they were sinners; that they were in need of God's mercy. They came to ask forgiveness of †Jesus. †Jesus was forgiving them. Their sin was being remitted. They were able to *"draw near"* to †Jesus both literally and spiritually.

In this parable †Jesus teaches us how unremitted sin is a barrier to God. The younger son left his father, walked away and squandered his inheritance in a sinful life. He chose to remain distant from his father. But, eventually, he longed to be with his father. First, however, he had to admit his sin. Finally, he realized he had sinned *"against heaven and against his father"*. *"So, he got up and went back to his father"*. By facing his father and asking forgiveness, he was able to draw closer to his father. His father put his arms around him and he was able to return to the home he had left.

It was a different story for the elder son. He did not enter the house but he remained at a distance; aloof from his father and his younger brother. The elder son could not see or admit to his own sin: his lack of compassion for his brother; his self-righteousness. The elder brother remained distant from his family.

These two brothers reveal what blocks us from closeness to †Jesus. Like the younger son, we allow sin to keep us away from God and, until we recognize our sin and ask forgiveness, we cannot draw near to God. Like the elder son, we often don't think we have any REAL sin. It's all those others who are sinners. We see the speck in the eye of others and we miss the plank in our own eye. The result is: we distance ourselves from the Father. The tax collectors and sinners drew near to †Jesus. The Scribes and Pharisees remained distant from †Jesus. They simply pointed fingers at those they believed were the real sinners; believing they were better.

In his Second Letter to the Corinthians, St. Paul writes, *"Whoever is a new creation, is in Christ"* (2 Corinthians 5: 17). Closeness to †Jesus comes when the old ways have passed and when we start off new. Unremitted sin is holding on to the old. †Jesus wants us to be close to Him, but WE must WANT it! Like the younger son we must face the Father and ask forgiveness. This is done in the sacrament of reconciliation. There are a couple of misconceptions that need to be cleared up. Contrary to popular belief, the Penitential Rite at the beginning of Mass does not absolve sins. The rite calls us to recognize our sinfulness and God's mercy. Also, self-forgiveness does not absolve sins; a self-confession. In the "Our Father", the prayer †Jesus taught us, we pray: *"Forgive us our trespasses..."* We are asking the Father to forgive us. This occurs in the Sacrament of Reconciliation, through the gift of Apostolic Succession. †Jesus instructed the Twelve; *"Whose sins you shall forgive they are forgiven"* (John 20:23). Sin not only damages us, it damages our relationship with God and, usually, with another. †Jesus is the mediator between us and the Father. The priest is "in persona Christi". Through the actions of the priest, sins are absolved. With a sincere and honest confession you can become a "new creation" as St. Paul proclaims. You get a "clean slate" as you return to the Father. The barrier that keeps us from †Jesus is removed; the barrier that keeps us from being part of the family of God. Bishop Giaquinta reminds us:

"Using the term 'family' for the Church is scriptural because the Bible refers to the Church as a bride (Eph. 5: 25-27; Rev. 21: 1-2, 9) and as a mother (LG #64). So we say with scriptural certainty that the Church is begotten as a family in the Cenacle. This beautiful doctrine need not languish at the level of speculation for it reveals the vitality of our relationship with God the Father; with †Jesus, our Brother; and with Mary, our mother. This teaching is the basis of our reciprocal rapport with one another as members of the Church". [xxix]

As we celebrate the Sacrament of Reconciliation the priest, in the person of Christ, brings you closer to the Father. It doesn't matter how long it's been since you have gone to confession, priests are joyful you have returned; just as the father in the parable was filled with joy when his younger son returned.

If you don't feel close to †Jesus, you have only yourself to blame. The Father is waiting for you to return home; to *"draw near"* to Him.

3. LOVE

Divine Agape

O Lord God, I love you above all things and
I love my neighbor for your sake because
you are the highest, infinite and perfect good,
worthy of all my love.
In this love I intend to live and die.
Amen.

Throughout the Gospels, †Jesus instructs His disciples to love one another:

"This is how all will know you are my disciples, if you have love for one another" (John 13:35).

This is not always easy; but it is do-able. †Jesus also tells them <u>how</u> they are to love one another:

"As I have loved you, so you should love one another" (John 13:34).

I don't know if this is so do-able. †Jesus loved to the point of death. Are we able to do that? Who do we love enough to die for: your spouse, children, a family member, a friend? †Jesus loved to the point of death for strangers! Looking at this criterion can we really be disciples of †Jesus?

After the Resurrection, †Jesus was to put this question to Peter:

> "'Simon, son of John, do you love me more than these?' He said to him, 'Yes, Lord, you know that I love you.' He said to him, 'Feed my lambs.' He then said to him a second time, 'Simon, son of John, do you love me?' He said to him, 'Yes, Lord, you know that I love you.' He said to him, 'Tend my sheep.' He said to him the third time, 'Simon, son of John, do you love me?' Peter was distressed that he had said to him a third time, 'Do you love me?' and he said to him, 'Lord, you know everything; you know that I love you.' (†Jesus) said to him, 'Feed my sheep'" (John 21: 15b-17).

†Jesus asks Peter: *"Do you love me?"* The Greek word used in this question is translated *"agape"*. It describes a self-less, perfect love. Peter replied to †Jesus: *"Yes, Lord, I love you"*. Peter's responds using a different Greek word for *"love"*: *"philos"*. This word describes an imperfect love. Peter was admitting to †Jesus that he could not love perfectly. †Jesus says to Peter: *"Feed my sheep"*.

A second time †Jesus asks: *"Peter, do you love me?"* Again, †Jesus uses the word *"agape"*. Peter replies: *"Yes, Lord, I love you"* (*philos*). †Jesus says to Peter: *"Feed my lambs"*. A third time †Jesus asks the question, this time using the word *"philos"*. *"Peter, do you love me (imperfectly)?"* Peter knows he can <u>only</u> love †Jesus imperfectly. After all, it was only a short time earlier that Peter had three times denied even knowing †Jesus. Peter responded to †Jesus: *"Lord, you know all things, you know I love you"*. *I can only love you philos (imperfectly).* †Jesus gives Peter his mission: *"Feed my sheep"*.

†Jesus knew Peter was not yet capable of Divine Agape: a faithful, selfless love. But still, †Jesus called Peter to discipleship. †Jesus called him to the fullness of love; to holiness. Eventually, Peter would express Divine Agape. It would be thirty years later in the Circus of Nero in Rome. Peter would give his life for the Gospel.

Let us return to the earlier verse in John's Gospel where †Jesus commands: *"As I have loved you, so should you love one another"* (John 13: 34). In this verse †Jesus uses the word *"agape"*. †Jesus makes it clear that the disciple is to imitate <u>His</u> love, a perfect, self-less. We are not to settle for a *"philos"* love. The call to holiness is a call to <u>Divine</u> <u>Agape</u>: a perfect, unselfish love. But, like Peter, most of us are not capable of that - yet. Does †Jesus reject us because we cannot accept the fullness of His call? NO! He still calls us to holiness; to discipleship. But, we are <u>not</u> off the hook. We must continually strive for Divine Agape. Our imperfect love must be transformed into a perfect love after the manner of †Jesus. Bishop Giaquinta reminds us:

"It is not enough to know the world...Let us learn from †Jesus how to love the world, from †Jesus who cries over the people of Jerusalem, 'Jerusalem, Jerusalem...how many times I have yearned to gather your children together...but you refused me' (Luke 13:34)! Let us learn from St Paul how to love our world. St. Paul, Christ's athlete and unbeatable warrior, had deep inner feelings of love and charity toward his brothers (and sisters)". xxx

In the Book of Revelation we read this:

"I, John, saw a new heaven and a new earth. The former heaven and the former earth had passed away" (Revelation. 21: 1-2).

Philos, imperfect love, exists in the former earth. Divine Agape is lived in *"the new heaven and new earth"*. This is where God dwells with His people.

"He will dwell with them and they will be His people and God, Himself, will always be with them" (Revelation. 21: 4).

Philos, imperfect love, is a human expression of love. But, †Jesus did not call us to be human. I have not found anywhere in the Sacred Scriptures where †Jesus says: *'You must be human as I am human'*. †Jesus called us to be holy. We do find this often in Sacred Scripture; the Old as well as the New Testament.

"You must be perfected as your heavenly Father is perfect" (Matthew. 5:48).

We are called to the perfection of love. We are called to Divine Agape. This must be the goal toward which we strive.

"The (Pro Sanctity) Movement's apostolic effectiveness and credibility will be judged in relation to the conviction its members show as they announce the message (of the universal call to holiness) with their lives. If they do not believe in or adhere to that which they announce, sooner or later, people will perceive their interior poverty.
"Therefore, it is fundamental, basic and essential to the Pro Sanctity apostolate that its members be individually and personally involved with their own call to holiness". xxxi

We must do more than talk the talk. Others will know whether or not we walk the walk. Just as Peter was called to bring his love for †Jesus to perfection, so are we.

What I am sharing with you is the Good News!!! †Jesus embraces us, †Jesus loves us. Even when our love is imperfect, His love for us remains Divinely Agape. †Jesus still calls us to be disciples; still calls us to be saints. But, there is even better news!!! †Jesus calls us to share in *"the new heavens and new earth"* (Revelations 21:1). †Jesus knows we are capable of Divine Agape. It is a matter of putting God first in my life. It demands that I remove self from self. We must trust in the power of the

Holy Spirit to help bring our love to perfection. Do not give up on Divine Agape. We must never throw our hands up in frustration and give up striving for holiness. In the Book of Revelation: *"The One who sits on the throne says: "Behold, I make all things new"* (Revelation 21: 5): philos to agape; sinner to saint; being human to being holy.

Our love is meant to mature from "philos" to "agape"; from an imperfect human love to a perfect, unselfish, sanctified love. To the degree we can embrace Divine Agape we will experience intimacy with God. †Jesus says:

"Whoever loves me will keep my word, and my Father (and I) will come to them, and make our dwelling place with them" (John 14: 23).

When, at the Last Supper, †Jesus speaks of sharing *"dwelling places"* with the Father, He is not referring to heavenly dwelling places. We all hope to be there someday. †Jesus promises an intimacy that is possible NOW; Heaven coming to us where we can experience the first rays of Resurrection; a Divine intimacy; a mystical marriage. †Jesus once said: *"The Kingdom is not here or there, the Kingdom is within you"*. But, most of the time we feel distant from God. We do not sense this closeness with our Divine Lover. Did †Jesus mean only certain people (saints) would experience this intimacy?

The Presence of God is in each one of us. However, most of us keep God on the periphery of our lives. Why don't we sense the presence of God; a deeper intimacy with the Lord? The answer is that we do not let Him into our inner rooms; into our heart. Our heart is too full of trivialities. I am too full of myself.

"We must absolutely avoid the worship of our own character. It is we who are to overcome the flaws of our character, without worrying about what others may be doing, whether or not they are truly trying to overcome themselves; it is we who must answer to God and to the Institute, on the effort we make or do not make to become vitally and practically, suitable for the little entity where the Lord has placed us". [xxxii]

It does not matter if that "little entity" is a particular Bethany (residence of consecrated Oblates), family or faith community. St. Teresa of Avila describes us as <u>Interior Castles.</u> There are different dwelling places within each of us. As we learn to love more selflessly the Lord is able to enter more deeply into our inner rooms. He eventually resides in our most interior room; the place where we will experience the deepest intimacy this side of heaven. St. Teresa calls this *Mystical Marriage.*

We have to admit, most Christians, maybe even us, keep †Jesus in the outer rooms. We want to be in control of our lives. We keep †Jesus at arm's length. That way, when we need the Lord we know exactly where to find Him: in that little box out there where we can invite Him in on

99

OUR terms. Most people are comfortable with †Jesus <u>out there.</u> Here, we tend to negotiate with God: *"Lord, I will do anything for you, but..."* We can take solace in the fact that at least God is part of our lives. We haven't shut the Lord out completely. But it is clear - I am the master of my castle. For this person, the spiritual life is based solely on a law and order morality: do's and don'ts: you shall do this; you shall not do that. Living by the Commandments will get you to heaven. But you will never experience Mystical Marriage in this life. Sure, we can live a respectable Christian life. But it is all about the externals. We live a false self - by impressions; what we want others to see. We want to control as much of our life as possible. Our love is fraternal, friendly, <u>philos</u>. But, our love is not sacrificial; selfless, <u>agape</u>. †Jesus is always a courteous guest. He will not go where He is not invited. He will not enter the inner dwelling places if I have closed them off to Him.

It is in the inner rooms where we will experience the intimate presence of the Lord. This can only happen when we lower the barriers and unlock the inner doors; when we open our heart to GOD'S WILL for us.

"It is not a matter of having or not having a strong will. Rather, it is a matter of developing the will and employing it for good...When we speak of detachment from the will, we mean that each of us must bend (their) will to the events of life and those who represent God". [xxxiii]

In other words, we must accept some of the things we experience in life (especially the crosses) as a pathway to a deeper relationship with God. Bishop Giaquinta reminds us:

"Here it would be well to remember that we continually strive, just as we pray in (the) 'Our Father', to find out the will of God and, when found, to carry it out". xxxiv

†Jesus tells His disciples: *"Do not let your hearts be troubled or afraid"* (John 14: 27). But we <u>are</u> afraid to let go of control; to trust God and surrender ourselves. A sign that we trust God is to listen and follow †Jesus.

"Whoever loves me will keep my word" (John 14: 23).

We tend to fill our inner rooms with worldly illusions. With the things our culture believes are important. The Word of God is meant to be counter-cultural. Our inner rooms should be reserved for Divine realities: Divine Agape; unselfish love, mercy, compassion. But, our hearts are too cluttered with what is not important. There is no room for both God and mammon.

"Behold, I stand at the door and knock. If anyone hears my voice and opens the door, (then) I will enter his house and dine with him" (Revelation 3:21).

†Jesus stands at the door and knocks. But, <u>we</u> have to let Him in. You might remember the famous painting of †Jesus standing at the door.

There is no door handle on His side. The door must be opened from within. St. Ambrose writes:

"Our soul has a door; it has gates. 'Lift up your hands, O gates, and be lifted up eternal gates, and the King of glory will enter'...Holiness too has its gates. We read in Scripture what the Lord †Jesus said, through the prophet: 'open for me the gates of holiness'.

"It is the soul that has its door, its gates. Christ comes to this door and knocks; He knocks at these gates. Open for Him; He wants to enter, to find his bride waiting and watching". xxxv

We must desire an intimate, loving relationship with †Jesus. Do we want our lives filled with the light and presence of the Father? Then we must empty our hearts of worldly distractions and desires. We must remove self from self. Bishop Giaquinta is clear on this point:

"The soul who is grounded in humility understands fully St. Paul's words by which He teaches us to esteem ourselves as the least of all creatures. (The soul) also understands the deep meaning of the little prayer of St. Therese of Lisieux...'May no one know me, may no one love me, may no one care about me; may they hold me in contempt and trample me underfoot like a grain of sand'". [xxxvi]

John the Baptist would declare: *"I must decrease and He must increase".*

Fr. Ron Rolheiser, in his book <u>A Holy Longing</u> [xxxvii] writes of the two functions of the soul. Our soul is not something <u>we</u> <u>have</u>, but more something <u>we</u> <u>are</u>. It is the very life-pulse within us, which makes us alive. We speak of someone dying precisely when the soul leaves the body. The soul is the life-principle within a human person. Our life-pulse, the soul has two functions. First, it is the principle of energy. There is only one body that is without energy or tension within it – a dead body. The soul is what gives us life. According to Rohlheiser, inside the soul lies the fire: the "eros", divine agape, the energy that drives us. It may sound strange to speak of "eros" in the same context of a love that leads to holiness. Pope Benedict XVI in his encyclical, <u>Deus</u> <u>Caritas</u> <u>Est</u>, writes that human "eros" is not repressed, but fulfilled in Divine Agape (selfless love). Pope Benedict attributes "eros" to God. God shares Himself, in Christ, to be passionate for mankind. Christ's free, self-gift reveals God's passion (desire) for communion with us; a passion that renders God vulnerable – even to death on the Cross.

The second function of the soul is to be an adhesive. It is the principle of integration and individuation within us. The soul holds us together. On the physical level, this is obvious. Biologically, we are an aggregate of chemicals. As long as we are alive, have a soul within us, these chemicals work together to form a single organism. At the moment of death, the chemicals go their own way. This is called <u>decomposition</u>. Chemicals which used to work together now do not. What is true bio-chemically is also true psychologically. The expression, *"to loose one's soul"* does not necessarily mean eternal damnation. It can mean, to become "unglued". I feel my inner world hopelessly crumbling, when I do not know who I am anymore. †Jesus said: *"What does it profit a person to gain the whole world and suffer the loss of his or her own soul?"* Could †Jesus be referring to losing my soul because I am trying to serve both *"God and mammon"* (Matthew 6: 24)? Am I living an ambivalent life? I am not united with God's will for me: to be holy.

A healthy soul must do two things for us. It must put some fire in our veins. Keeping us energized, vibrant, living with zest and full of hope. When this breaks down, something is wrong with our soul. When cynicism, despair, bitterness or depression paralyzes our energy, part of the soul is hurting. A healthy soul also has to keep us put together. It continually gives us a sense of who we are, where we came from, and where we are going. It helps us makes sense of life. A healthy soul, unites us to the Father, through †Jesus Christ, in the Holy Spirit. A healthy soul possesses the Fire of Divine Love. It is God's Spirit, God's creative love that lives within us. It is the holiness of God in which we live, and move and have our being. Do I live with a passion for God and for the things of God? Do I have a desire for sanctity? We must not worry about impressing others; being accepted or popular. What must be our vocation, is expressing Divine Agape. The doors of our inner dwelling places must be opened wide for Christ: His way, His truth, His Life. Then, we will find, as we read in the Book of Revelation:

"There is no need of sun or moon to shine on (our interior dwelling places), for the glory of God gives it light, and its lamp is (Christ)" (Rev. 21: 23).

Love And Mission

O †Jesus, divine model of sanctity, who
by Your example, even before Your words,
showed us the perfection of the Father as a
goal, we, who are gathered here at Your feet,
want to meditate again today on your invitation
to love and our duty to respond to it.
And, if it was not love, what else was Your life,
from the poverty in the cave to nakedness on
the cross?
But all this You bore, O Lord, to make us
understand what loves means and remember
at the same time, the essence of perfection
found therein.
Many times You repeated to us that only in You
true peace is to be found. Truly, only in You
is contained the source of divine water, that
quenches our thirst and comforts us, until it
becomes in us a fountain that springs up to
eternal life.

(+G. Giaquinta)

There was an important controversy in the early
Church. It centered around this question: was †Jesus

divine or human? Was †Jesus true God or true man? It came to be known as the heresy of adoptionism. The theory stated that, because of the good life †Jesus lived, †Jesus, the man, was adopted by God as God's son. There were other early Gnostic heresies. One believed that God had slipped into a human shell. That God had paraded around as a man. God was wearing a human costume. He really did not suffer on the cross. After all, God was not truly human.

A Council was called to discern the truth of the divinity and humanity of Christ. This was the Council of Nicea in 325 A.D. After prayer and discernment, the Council declared: †Jesus has two equal natures: human and divine. The two natures of †Jesus are inseparable and alike. The Greek word used to express this truth was "homousios"; it was translated: "of the same substance". Thus, we believe that †Jesus is: "True God and True Man".

Let us look at the Gospel of Matthew. This Gospel was written over two centuries before the Council of Nicea. When asked by a scholar of the Law, a Pharisee, about the greatest commandment, †Jesus teaches the two great Commandments of the Law:

"You shall love the Lord, your God, with all your heart, with all your soul, and with all your mind. This is the greatest and the first Commandment. The second is like it: You shall love your neighbor as yourself" (Matthew 22: 36-40).

The Greek word Matthew uses for *"like it"*: is *homousios.* It is the same word used two centuries later at the Council of Nicea. What is †Jesus teaching us? The love of God and love of neighbor are inseparable; they are of the same substance. As †Jesus is truly God and truly man, we cannot love God and <u>not</u> our neighbor. Despise your neighbor, you despise God. If you cheat your neighbor, you cheat God. When you hurt others, you disrespect God. This was the intention of the original Commandments.

"You shall not wrong any widow or orphan. If you ever wrong them and they cry out to me, I will surely hear their cry" (Exodus 22: 21).

After †Jesus taught the greatest Commandment, three chapters later in Matthew's Gospel, †Jesus sits on the Mount of Olives with His disciples. He reveals to them, who their neighbor is; the one they are to love as themselves.

"When I was <u>hungry</u>, you gave me food, I was <u>thirsty</u> and you gave me drink, a <u>stranger</u> and you welcomed me, <u>naked</u> and you clothed me, <u>ill</u> and you cared for me, in <u>prison</u> and you visited me..." (Matthew 25).

Love of these neighbors and love of God is the same; they are inseparable. We cannot separate the sacred from the secular. We cannot compartmentalize our faith life and our daily life. We cannot separate our relationship with God from our relationships with others. I cannot separate my faith, hope and love of God from the presence of God who dwells in every person. When I disrespect or dishonor my spouse, I have done the same to God. When I disrespect and dishonor those with legitimate authority over me, I have done the same to God. When I say hateful things about another, I have said them about God. If I live an unchaste life, I have been unfaithful to God. If I am selfish toward others, I am selfish with God.

St Paul reminds us in his First Letter to the Thessalonians:

"Be imitators of the Lord...a model for all the believers" (1 Thessalonians 1: 6-7).

We imitate the Lord by embracing our call to holiness; by loving after the manner of †Jesus. We are to live by the First Commandment: to love God with all that we are. Even to love Him with what we are not and have yet to become through His grace. The second Commandment is like it; it is the same as the first: To love others as we love ourselves. If we possess a self-loathing or self-hatred, we cannot possibly love our neighbor as †Jesus commands. We cannot possibly love God as He calls us. We are to treat others as we would want to be treated; even if our neighbor treats us poorly. Bishop Giaquinta writes:

"We will not relent in helping our neighbor, even when we see in them more human elements than the image of the Creator. We will discover the image of God in them, perhaps marred and distorted, or perhaps made even unrecognizable by passions and sin. Our supernatural vision – which is not ruled by either affinity, aversion or a purely human estimation – will be able to see in our neighbor's soul what human eyes are unable to see". [xxxviii]

If we live with this spiritual vision, there is no end to the blessings we can receive. We will show the world that we are children of God. We will witness to the divine indwelling of the Holy Spirit alive within us. We will know and understand that nothing separates us from the love of God (Romans 8: 39).

The Sacred Scriptures are a testament to God's love for us, in fact, two Testaments of God's love for us. It is the divinely revealed witness to the unconditional fullness of God's love. It is also a divinely revealed itinerary for the journey to holiness: imitating the love of God.

In the New Testament, originally written in Greek, we find various Greek words for love. Let us review.

- o *Philos*: a love between friends.
- o *Storg'e*: a love among family members.
- o *Eros*: a love that desires to possess what I lack. This includes a yearning for union with another.
- o *Agape*: this is the most familiar Greek word for love among Christians. It describes a self-

giving love of one who seeks, exclusively, the good of another. A completely self-less love. God's love for us is described as *Agape*.

The call to holiness is real <u>only</u> when there is a desire for conversion, when there is a willingness to surrender myself to God. There must be a desire to purify what is disordered in my Christian life. A question to ask yourself is this: "What kind of love must I have, to more fully imitate †Jesus? To be holy as He is holy?" As we explore the Scriptures we find different expressions of love; Love that imitates the perfect love of God.

Recall in the First Book of Samuel.

"In those days, Saul went down to the desert of Ziph with three thousand picked men of Israel, to search for David in the desert of Ziph. So David and Abishai went among Saul's soldiers by night and found Saul lying asleep within the barricade, with his spear thrust into the ground at his head and Abner and his men sleeping around him.

Abishai whispered to David: "God has delivered your enemy into your grasp this day. Let me nail him to the ground with one thrust of the spear; I will not need a second thrust!" But David said to Abishai, "Do not harm him, for who can lay hands on the LORD's anointed and remain unpunished?" (1 Samuel 26: 2, 7-9).

David had the opportunity to kill Saul. Why shouldn't David take his life? King Saul was trying to kill him. David stood over Saul with his spear. Abishai, one of David's soldiers said: "Do it! Now is your chance". But David did not kill Saul. He loved and respected God too much. David replies: *"Who am I to lay hands on the Lord's anointed?"* (1 Samuel 26: 9). Even though Saul had turned from God, Saul no longer enjoyed God's favor or that of the people. But, Saul had been anointed by God to be king. For David to have taken Saul's life would have been a violation of God's choice. How many of us have the restraint of David? I am sure we would not kill someone; at least not with a spear. But we are willing to do so with our words. We destroy another's reputation by what we say through gossip or mean-spirited criticism; comments that are meant to humiliate or embarrass another. Don't we realize that they are loved by God as much as we are? That they are His children, His anointed?

It is our obligation, as Apostles of Holiness, to care for them as we would want them to do for us; to care for them as God cares for them; as we would care for †Jesus, the Blessed Mother, the saints. They are part of our spiritual family. They are members of the Mystical Body of Christ as we are. Bishop Giaquinta taught;

"It seems to me that the practical and most significant way of living out this program of ours is summed up in that most dear and most noted formula 'Sentire cum Ecclesia' (to be of one heart with the Church). We must be aware of the reality of the mystical Body, not as a vague or abstract reality, but of something of which we are a part. Perhaps we occupy its lowest place, or perhaps we are its most insignificant part, but still we wish to live intimately united with this immense family, with this Body that is †Jesus living through the centuries". [xxxix]

We must express a more *storg'e* love. We must recognize that we are all part of the Mystical Body of Christ. This is a love that expresses our unity as a family of Love. What Bishop Giaquinta called the Second Dimension of Holiness.

"We are a family born from love, in which one must live with love toward the Father - live, that is, a life of holiness - a life whose inner relationships are as among brothers (and sisters), and must be regulated by love". [xl]

Bishop Giaquinta also reminds us that we cannot ignore the spiritual formation of others. It is our responsibility. It is an expression of fraternal, *storg'e* love.

In Psalm 103 we read:

"As far as the east is from the west, so far has God put our transgressions from us" (Psalm 103: 12).

God is infinitely merciful and loving. Regardless of how often we disobey or reject the Lord He always offers us the chance to reconcile. When someone hurts us, are we willing to forgive and forget? Yes, we may bury the hatchet, but you can be sure we will mark the spot. Yet, every time we celebrate the Sacrament of Reconciliation the words of this Psalm become real. Sacramental absolution brings a clean slate; a new beginning. *"As far as the east is from the west"*... (Psalm 103:12). That is where God puts our sins. Our God is a God of new beginnings. Why? Because **there is hope for everyone!** In the

Sacrament of Reconciliation, God expresses *Agape* and *Philos*. God is willing to forgive AND forget. †Jesus said to His disciples:

"I no longer call you slaves, because a slave does not know what his master is doing. I call you friends, because I have told you everything I heard from my Father" (John 15: 15).

Bishop Giaquinta writes:

"The (Pro Sanctity) Movement's apostolic effectiveness and credibility will be judged in relation to the conviction its members show as they announce the message with their lives. If they do not believe in or adhere to that which they announce, sooner or later, people will perceive their interior poverty". [xli]

Others will know if we are all <u>show</u> <u>and</u> <u>tell</u>. They will know that we are not truly committed to the call to holiness.

In the Gospel of Luke we read:

"Do unto others as you would have them do unto you...Forgive and you will be forgiven" (Luke 6: 31-37).

Our culture has corrupted the Golden Rule: "Do unto others BEFORE they do it to you". "Don't give, but take before it is taken from you". †Jesus said: *"Love your enemies, do good to those who hate you"* (Luke 6: 27). Our culture teaches: "Don't show weakness and don't turn the other cheek; get even". Bishop Giaquinta calls us to a radical generosity:

"A generosity that knows how to practice the Gospel teaching, 'when someone strikes you on the right cheek, turn the other one to him' (Matt. 5:39). This is what †Jesus taught us. However, we know all too well how He first practiced what He later taught (Acts 1:1). If †Jesus could say that His disciple's detachment must be complete, it is only because He first lived such detachment Himself". xlii

†Jesus taught us how to treat those who hate us. The events of Good Friday present us with the lesson we must never forget. He prayed for them from the Cross. Now, we won't have to pray while nailed to a cross, but, simply on our knees, or in our favorite chair. Is †Jesus asking too much of us?

"We must expect from ourselves more than we can possibly demand from others...We must live out our program of spiritual life...with integrity". xliii

I was at a meeting of clergy; Cardinal Mahoney was there. A group of survivors of clergy abuse were outside protesting; condemning the Cardinal and the clergy. During our Mass, the Cardinal encouraged us not to be angry about the slurs and comments. But simply pray for those abused by priests. This is *storg'e* love: praying for all members of God's family even when they hate us.

116

I return to the question I asked earlier: "What kind of love must I have, to more fully imitate †Jesus? To be holy as He is holy?"? What kind of love is necessary for holiness: All four kinds of love that are revealed in Scripture.

Philos: to love others as brothers and sisters in Christ. This love is sometimes expressed as fraternal correction. Bishop Giaquinta reminds us that "correction is an apostolic act". [xliv]

Storg'e: to love everyone as members of the mystical family of God. We are all children of God.

Agape: to be completely selfless toward others.

Eros: no, I didn't make a mistake. Yes, it can be a selfish, imperfect form of love. But, God's love is also expressed as *Eros*. Pope Benedict XVI reminded us of this in his message to the Church, during Lent of 2007. *Eros* is a love that desires to possess what it lacks. It is a love that yearns for union with the beloved.

"Christ 'draws himself to me' in order to unite Himself to me, so I can learn to love my brothers and sisters with His own love". [xlv]

On the cross, †Jesus yearned for us with an insatiable thirst.

"The dying †Jesus, through His parched lips, uttered a word that was derided by the soldiers and poorly interpreted by those with just a human sense of compassion, but that for us implies an invitation to feel the need to seek out people – the same need that provoked †Jesus' painful THIRST (John. 19: 28)". [xlvi]

†Jesus wants to possess our divided hearts. He wants us completely. †Jesus yearns for union with us. Do you think it is too much to give †Jesus what He asks for? Bishop Giaquinta did not think so:

"As we cannot turn a deaf ear to this cry of the Master, so we cannot turn a deaf ear to the other imploring cry of people in search of help. People are turning to us for help as they once turned to St. Paul, 'Come and save us' (Acts 16: 9). Let us remember that our brothers and sisters expect to be saved by us, and that their damnation or eternal blessedness will depend, perhaps, on one of our acts of generosity". [xlvii]

These words of Bishop Giaquinta are a reminder of our call. It is not only a call to *"love the Lord, your God, with all your heart, with all your soul, and with all your mind...You shall love your neighbor as yourself"* (Matthew 22: 36-40). It is also a universal call to holiness. It is a call to mission! Our life is mission!

We follow in the footsteps of the Apostles and the first community of Christians gathered together on that first Pentecost. We recall the Holy Spirit descending on the first followers of †Jesus. They had gathered together in the Cenacle, following the instructions of †Jesus. With the coming of the Holy Spirit they are given the courage of their conviction: that †Jesus is Lord and Messiah. They are given the gift to proclaim this truth to the world through the gift of a variety of language; sharing their faith with others. They were to carry on the mission of †Jesus to the ends of the earth. †Jesus commissioned them after the Resurrection:

"Go, therefore, and make disciples of all nations, baptizing in the name of the Father, and of the Son, and of the Holy Spirit. Teaching them to observe all I have commanded you...And behold, I am with you always until the end of the age" (Matthew 28: 19-20).

†Jesus sent His Spirit so the disciples would have the gifts to complete the mission.

With these Scriptures, we are doing more than simply remembering an historical event. It is a reminder of our call: *We are the Body of Christ. Our life is mission.* To spread the "Good News" was not limited to those gathered in that upper room on that day in Jerusalem. It is not only for the ordained or vowed. It is not only for laity who have the time; who don't have careers or large families. All of us are called to participate in the mission of Christ – WHY? *We are the Body of Christ. Our life is mission.*

Through Baptism, we have all received the same Holy Spirit as those first disciples in Jerusalem. We have been given gifts of the Spirit enabling us to participate in the mission of †Jesus.

"There are different kinds of spiritual gifts but the same Spirit...to each individual the manifestation of the Spirit is given for some benefit" (1 Corinthians 12: 4-8).

We are expected to use these gifts; to use them responsibly and generously to build up the Body of Christ. We have been given the Spirit of Christ to continue His work of redemption. St. Paul reminds us:

"I rejoice in my sufferings for your sake, and in my flesh I am filling up what is lacking in the afflictions of Christ on behalf of His body, which is the Church" (Colossians 1: 24).

By the power of the Spirit, *we are the Body of Christ. Our life is Mission.* The mission is to be the face of †Jesus in the world. St. Paul writes: *"We behold the glory of the Lord with unveiled faces; that glory which comes from the Lord who is the Spirit, transforms us all into His likeness".* What face of †Jesus have you been given? Are you the face of the servant †Jesus? Who knows that the *"last shall be first"?* Who chooses *"to serve rather than be served"?* Are you the face of the welcoming †Jesus; opening your heart to all people; inviting God's poor, little ones? Are you the face of the forgiving †Jesus; rich in mercy and full of kindness? Are you the face of the compassionate †Jesus; able to participate in the sufferings of others? Are you the face of †Jesus the teacher; passing on His truth in your words and actions? Are you the face of the simple †Jesus; carrying one staff and one pair of sandals? We are, collectively, the face of †Jesus. *We are the Body of Christ. Our life is mission.*

The face of †Jesus is manifested in a variety of ways through the Spirit of †Jesus.

"There are different forms of service but one Lord; there are different workings of the same God who produces all of them in everyone" (1 Corinthians 12: 5-6).

All the Baptized possess a likeness to Christ. We all have been given a face of †Jesus. All the various manifestations of the Spirit are expressions of <u>Divine</u> <u>Agape</u>. The love expressed by †Jesus.

"Whoever loves me will keep my word, and my Father will love him, and we will come to them and make our dwelling with them" (John 14: 23).

St. Paul writes of our unity as the Body of Christ, the different gifts and the different forms of service in Chapter 12 of his First Letter to the Corinthians. In the very next chapter, he provides the criteria for expressing the face of †Jesus.

"If I speak in human and angelic tongues but do not have love, I am a resounding gong or a clashing cymbal...

If I give away everything I own, and if I hand my body over so that I may boast but do not have love, I gain nothing.

Love is patient, love is kind. It is not jealous, (love) is not pompous, it is not inflated, it is not rude, it does not seek its own interests, it is not quick-tempered, it does not brood over injury,

it does not rejoice over wrongdoing but rejoices with the truth.

It bears all things, believes all things, hopes all things, endures all things.

Love never fails...

So faith, hope, love remain, these three; but the greatest of these is love" (1 Corinthians 13: 1-13).

It is <u>in</u> our love...that the face of †Jesus is revealed. It is <u>by</u> our love...that the mission of †Jesus continues. It is <u>through</u> our love...that our true self is revealed: to be holy as God is Holy. It is when we love, that we witness to the world: *We are the Body of Christ. Our life is mission.* Our mission is to proclaim with our voices and with our lives...The universal call to holiness.

Fullness of Love

Every Good Friday, we hear these words proclaimed from the Passion of †Jesus: *"I thirst"*. †Jesus is not crying out for water. †Jesus is thirsting for our love. In his Lenten message of 2007, Pope Benedict XVI wrote:

"On the cross, it is God Himself who begs the love of His creature. He is thirsty for the love of every one of us."

Now is a time for conversion and renewal. What is it we hope to renew: Our love for God. Love for God is diminished with every sin, with every act of selfishness. Now is the time to ask forgiveness for our <u>lack</u> of love, to seek renewal of our <u>lost</u> love, to open our hearts to receive the <u>unconditional</u> love of God. We are called to the fullness of love – Divine Agape; to love God, our neighbor and ourselves. Without all three, human love is incomplete.

The call to the fullness of love was the message of the Sermon on the Mount. Beginning with the Beatitudes and includes our Gospel today. †Jesus gives us a spiritual itinerary for the renewal of our life and loves: love of God, neighbor and self:

"When you pray, go to your inner room...and pray to your Father in secret" (see Matthew 6: 5ff).

The purpose of prayer is NOT to get something. The purpose of prayer is relationship; to deepen my relationship with God. Love grows in any relationship through dialogue and communication. No one falls in love through silence. Love only happens by getting to know the other person. The *"inner room"* †Jesus speaks of is the heart. We read in the Book of the Prophet Joel:

"Even now, says the Lord, return to me with your whole heart" (Joel 2: 12).

Through these reflections we have had the opportunity to return to our inner room. There, we have, hopefully, found God. We have fallen in love with Him all over again - or maybe, for the first time.

"When you give alms...do not let your right hand know what your left hand is doing" (see Matthew 6: 1ff).

To give alms, is to express generosity to another. To give alms is to love the †Jesus we see in others. Love of God, without love of neighbor, is hypocrisy. You cannot have one without the other. They are of the same substance just as the human and divine natures of †Jesus is part of the one person of Christ. Almsgiving is not only about giving money, it is giving myself. Almsgiving is expressing love to my neighbor whether I know my neighbor or not. Almsgiving can take many forms: giving my precious time to help another, patiently listening to someone's story, putting aside something that gives me pleasure, to help another. Anytime I give of myself, for another, it is a form of almsgiving; it is to be †Jesus to another. St. Paul writes in his Second Letter to the Corinthians:

"We are ambassadors of Christ, as if God were appealing through us" (2 Corinthians 5: 20).

Be generous with alms; be generous with yourself. Bring the unconditional love of Christ to all you meet. Bishop Giaquinta reminds us:

"Love does not care only for big things but also pauses for the details with maternal tenderness. Christian love gives everything, as †Jesus gave His life, it extends itself to everyone, as †Jesus forgave on the Cross....It is a love that (radiates) divine love; to do good to everyone, to leave a trace of God in everyone". [xlviii]

When was the last time you left a trace of God in someone? This should be a daily goal of our vocation.

"When you fast, anoint your head and wash your face" (see Matthew 6: 16ff).

To understand fasting, only in terms of food is to limit this important discipline of the spiritual life. Fasting is meant to restore the spiritual balance in my life; to restore a healthy <u>love</u> <u>of</u> <u>self</u>. To have a healthy love of self means to desire all the grace the Holy Spirit wants to pour out upon me. It is to desire my greatest good – holiness. It is to desire to be ONE with God. Pope St. Leo the Great reminds us that before we fast from food, we should fast from sin. It is turning away from sin that leads to my highest calling – holiness. This is why, when we administer ashes on Ash Wednesday, we pray: "Turn away from sin, and be faithful to the Gospel".

We read in Psalm 51: *"A clean heart create for me, O God, and a steadfast spirit renew within me"* (vs. 12). The call to holiness requires that we fast from that which corrupts the soul; that which diminishes the Spirit within us. Love and respect the Temple of the Holy Spirit that you are. This is how we express, love of self.

To embrace the fullness of love is the goal the Universal Call to Holiness. To deepen my love for God, through prayer; to deepen my love for others, through the giving of alms – the giving of myself; to deepen love for myself, by fasting from sin. This will involve sacrifice. There can be no spiritual renewal without sacrifice. Whatever you do, whatever path you take it should lead you to the fullness of love. Pope Benedict XVI wrote:

"Let us look at Christ pierced on the cross...He is thirsty for the love of every one of us...Many of the saints found in the heart of †Jesus the deepest expression of this mystery of love". [xlix]

The deepest expression of the mystery of love, the fullness of love – Divine Agape, will make us holy as God is holy.

CONCLUSION

Desire and Design for Holiness

We are part of a larger family. "We are the Body of Christ - Our life is mission." St. Paul reminds us in his First Letter to the Corinthians (chapter 12): the Body of Christ has many parts. Distributed throughout the parts are a variety of charisms. Charisms are essential for the health and spiritual benefit of the entire Body; for the good of the Body of Christ; for the glory and honor of God. The Holy Spirit would not have given charisms if it was not essential for the health and maturity of the Body of Christ. These charism are essential to the Body of Christ. God has revealed and given us charism at this moment in Salvation History because it is crucial to His divine plan. We are small – but not insignificant. We are leaven; we are the mustard seed! We are a *"pearl of great price"* to †Jesus. We are vital to His Mystical Body. Bishop Giaquinta writes:

"A profoundly sacred vision emerges when we think of the Church as a family...The parish should exist as a family with the priest at the center; the Diocese is like a large family around the Bishop; the whole Church is an immense family with the Bishop of Bishops, the Pope, at the center...These various realities should be motivated by a relationship of intimacy, reciprocal assistance, fraternal understanding, family affection and, even more, the affection characteristic of the supernatural family". [1]

At the foundation of this universal family, that Bishop Giaquinta writes of is every Catholic household. The Utopia of Saints that he dreamed of begins in each home. This Utopia seems an impossible dream. But it is not; it has already existed once. We need only reflect on the lives of Mary, Joseph and †Jesus: the Holy Family.

From the Annunciation to Mary's visit to Elizabeth; the journey from Nazareth to Bethlehem; the birth of †Jesus and His presentation in the Temple; their flight into Egypt; and twelve years later, †Jesus talking with the religious scholars in the Temple; the public ministry of †Jesus, His paschal mystery and Mary's presence in the early Church; in every circumstance of life, †Jesus, Mary and Joseph expressed the fullness of love. Tradition has called this family, Holy. And so they were. While we admire them, even envy them, most don't believe they can be imitated. After all – they were the *Holy Family*. Our families are dysfunctional. Community life can be so difficult. In truth, we are all capable of holiness; capable of creating holy families and holy communities. A "culture of holiness" as Catarina, the General Moderator of the Apostolic Oblates wrote:

"...We are journeying toward holiness, striving to build a 'culture of holiness' in a holier and more fraternal world, as our Founder teaches us". [li]

It is a matter of <u>desire</u> and <u>design</u>.

We are already <u>designed</u> for holiness. It is in our hard-wiring. In the Book of Genesis, we read in the Creation story:

"God created man <u>in</u> <u>his</u> <u>image</u>; in the <u>divine</u> <u>image</u> he created him; male and female He created them" (Genesis 1: 27).

God is holy. And if we share in His image, we are <u>designed</u> for holiness from the very beginning of life. In the Book of Leviticus: The Lord gives instructions to the Israelites:

"You shall be holy, because I am holy" (11:44).

God would not ask them to be something they were not capable of becoming. God has <u>designed</u> us for holiness. In the Sermon in the Mount †Jesus says:

"You must be perfected as you heavenly Father is perfect" (Matthew 5: 48).

Obviously †Jesus believed perfection, holiness, is within our grasp; it is possible. We are <u>designed</u> for holiness. The Second Vatican Council teaches:

"All Christian, regardless of the rank or state in life, are called to holiness". [lii]

It is our vocation as Christians. We are <u>designed</u> by God for holiness. Here is the problem: we don't have a strong desire to be holy. It is too difficult to create holy families; holiness demands being counter-cultural. It is so much easier to let the media baby-sit the children rather than helping the design of God to grow within them. It is much less stressful to ignore a member of my family rather than work out our differences and mature in self-less love. It is easier not to deal with the "elephant in the room". We seem to lack the <u>desire</u> for holiness. What is necessary to embrace the desire? We must have a *Desirous Heart* for holiness.

The Holy Family shows us how to desire holiness. Prayer was at the heart of their family life. Mary could respond to the angel's voice because she was a woman of prayer. Joseph recognized his dreams as coming from God, because he had a prayerful relationship with God. †Jesus was constantly at prayer; seeking the guidance of "Abba". Holiness and prayerfulness go hand in hand. They are necessary in developing holy families.

<u>Docility</u> was the core of their life as a family. Obediently listening to God's will. Saying "yes" without completely understanding how God's will, would unfold; "pondering" the issues of everyday life. They chose to live with the tensions of striving for holiness in an increasingly secular world. They trusted that the Lord's words to them would be fulfilled. They were obedient to rabbinic teaching.

"They fulfilled all the prescriptions of the Law of Moses" (cf. Luke 2: 22).

They were faithful to Jewish Law. They never claimed to know better because of some special enlightenment or special privilege. From the Annunciation to the Crucifixion they were docile to God's will.

They were <u>supportive</u> of one another's vocation. Joseph chose not to divorce Mary. Rather, he trusted her vocation as the mother of the Savior. †Jesus changed water into wine when Mary requested this at her friend's wedding. Even though †Jesus was not ready to manifest himself. Mary followed †Jesus to Jerusalem even when she preferred to protect Him in the safety of Nazareth. But Mary surrendered <u>her</u> <u>will</u> to support <u>His</u> <u>mission</u>.

They were <u>willing</u> <u>to</u> <u>sacrifice</u> for the good of one another; even when it meant relocating to Egypt to escape Herod. Mary was to suffer a heart pierced by a sword out of love for God and for her vocation as the mother of †Jesus. †Jesus would sacrifice His life for us: His brothers and sisters.

Desire and Design for Holiness. One is our work. One is God's work. But even our desire is made possible by God's grace. A priest once asked Mother Teresa: "How can I be Holy?" She responded: "If you have the desire, God will do the rest" [liii] (Rev. Anthony Figueiredo; "At the

School of the Mother: The Marian Spirituality of John Paul II; Behold Your Mother; ed. By Stephen J. Rossetti; Ave Maria Press, 2007). How do we recognize the desire for holiness? By living as St. Paul describes:

"...with heartfelt compassion, kindness, humility, gentleness, patience and mutual forgiveness; with gratitude to God in our heart" (Colossians 3: 12-13).

It is by being prayerful and docile; obedient to God's will and teaching authority of the Church; supportive of one another's vocation; by loving sacrificially.

Holiness in family life is possible for us all. Whatever form your family takes: traditional, incomplete by divorce or the death of a family member, single, vowed or consecrated or part of the ordained community. It demands mutual support of each member's vocation. To build up one another; not demeaning one another out of jealousy or indifference to them. Who are we to dismiss the handiwork of God in one another? We must have the desire to live out the design, to support one another in living out the vocation to holiness. We are designed in the image of God: holy as He is holy.

It is not for me to have the last word in this book. I am of no importance. Rather, we will conclude with the words of the Servant of God, Bishop Giaquinta, calling us to desire holiness:

"We must first of all have zeal. †Jesus borrowed words from the Psalm to describe Himself: '...zeal for your house consumes me' (Ps. 68:10)...The more (we) devote (ourselves) to the apostolate (of living and proclaiming the call to holiness) the more (we) will feel this burning love for God and for souls. This love shall not be intimidated by failure but will be inventive and creative in leading others to the Lord". [liv]

End Notes

[i] From L'Osservatore Romano; English edition; No. 30; 27 July 2005.

[ii] Giaquinta; Formation and Apostolate; 2nd printing, 1972; p. 10-11.

[iii] (Giaquinta; Formation and Apostolate; 2nd printing, 1972; p. 5-6).

[iv] (Giaquinta; Program of Spiritual Life; 3rd Ed., 2004; p. 34).

[v] (Giaquinta; Program of Spiritual Life; 3rd Ed., 2004; p. 48).

[vi] (Castle VII, 4:12).

[vii] (Giaquinta; Formation and Apostolate; 2nd printing, 1972; p.3).

[viii] (Giaquinta; Program of Spiritual Life; 3rd edition; July, 2004; p. 20).

[ix] (Giaquinta; Program of Spiritual Life; 3rd edition; July, 2004; p. 18-19).

[x] (Giaquinta; Program of Spiritual Life; 3rd edition; July, 2004; p. 61-62).

[xi] (Giaquinta; Formation and Apostolate; Second English edition, 1973; p. 12).

[xii] (Giaquinta; "The Gifts of the Holy Spirit"; Retreat led in Rome, May 31-June 4, 1958).

[xiii] (St. Anthony of Padua; Sermons for the Easter Cycle; George Marcel, OFM, editor; 1994; p. 102).

[xiv] (Giaquinta; The Cenacle; 2nd Edition, 1992; pp. 49-51).

[xv] (Giaquinta; The Spirituality of the Pro Sanctity Movement; 1980; P. 34-35).

[xvi] (Benedict XVI; Homily, 19 October 2006).

[xvii] (Giaquinta; Program of Spiritual Life; 3rd Edition, 2004; P. 187).

[xviii] (LG, 40.2).

[xix] (John Paul II; Ecclesia in America, 1, 26, 66).

[xx] (Giaquinta; "The Gifts of the Holy Spirit"; Retreat led in Rome, May 31 – June 4, 1958).

[xxi] (Giaquinta; "To Become Gift"; Retreat Given October 31 – November 4, 1962; Outline 12, Chapter 3, Third Day).

[xxii] (Teresa of Avila; Life 7:17.b).

[xxiii] (Giaquinta; Formation and Apostolate; 2nd Edition; 1973).

xxiv (Giaquinta; <u>Program</u> <u>of</u> <u>Spiritual</u> <u>Life</u>; 3rd Edition; July, 2004; p. 185).

xxv (Retreat; 16 July 1982)

xxvi (Letter; June 2006)

xxvii (Retreat; 19 July 1982).

xxviii (Retreat; 21 July 1982).

xxix (Giaquinta; <u>The Cenacle</u>; Second Edition, 2003; p. 66-67).

xxx (Giaquinta; <u>Program</u> <u>of</u> <u>Spiritual</u> <u>Life</u>'; Third Edition; July, 2004; p. 19).

xxxi (Giaquinta; <u>The</u> <u>Spirituality</u> <u>of</u> <u>the</u> <u>Pro</u> <u>Sanctity</u> <u>Movement</u>; p. 78).

xxxii (Giaquinta; <u>Program</u> <u>of</u> <u>Spiritual</u> <u>Life</u>; Third Edition; July, 2004; p. 70).

xxxiii (Giaquinta; <u>Program</u> <u>of</u> <u>Spiritual</u> <u>Life</u>; Third Edition; July, 2004; p. 71-72).

xxxiv (Giaquinta; <u>Program</u> <u>of</u> <u>Spiritual</u> <u>Life</u>; Third Edition; July, 2004; p. 71-72).

xxxv (St. Ambrose; from and exposition on Psalm 118; cf: Liturgy of the Hours; Office of Readings; Thursday, 14th Week in Ordinary Time).

xxxvi (Giaquinta; <u>Program of Spiritual Life</u>; Third Edition; July, 2004; p. 79).

xxxvii (Doubleday, 1999).

xxxviii (Giaquinta: <u>Program of Spiritual Life</u>; Third edition; July, 2004; p. 183).

xxxix (Giaquinta; <u>Program of Spiritual Life</u>; 3rd ed., 2004; p. 39).

xl (Giaquinta,: <u>Love is a Revolution</u>, Pro Sanctity Edition, Rome, 1973, p.172.

xli (Giaquinta; <u>The Spirituality of the Pro Sanctity Movement</u>; p. 78).

xlii (Giaquinta; <u>Program of Spiritual Life</u>; 3rd Ed., 2004; p. 35).

xliii (Giaquinta; <u>Program of Spiritual Life</u>; 3rd Ed., 2004; p. 39).

xliv (<u>Program of Spiritual Life</u>; p. 42).

xlv (Pope Benedict XVI; Lenten Message; 2007).

xlvi (Giaquinta; <u>Program for Spiritual Life</u>; 3rd ed., 2004; p. 43).

xlvii (Giaquinta; <u>Program of Spiritual Life</u>; 3rd ed.' p. 43).

xlviii (Giaquinta; <u>Formation and Apostolate</u>; 2nd printing, 1975; pp.

14-15).

xlix (Pope Benedict XVI, 2007 Lenten Message).

l (Giaquinta; The Spirituality of the Pro Sanctity Movement; p.68-69).

li (Letter of 6 August 2007).

lii (Lumen Gentium, 40.2).

liii (Rev. Anthony Figueiredo; "At the School of the Mother: The Marian Spirituality of John Paul II; Behold Your Mother; ed. By Stephen J. Rossetti; Ave Maria Press, 2007).

liv (Giaquinta; Program for Spiritual Life; 3rd edition; July, 2004; p. 181).